CINCINNATI'S LITERARY HERITAGE

A History for Booklovers

KEVIN GRACE

THE History PRESS

Published by The History Press
Charleston, SC
www.historypress.com

All images from the author's private collection unless otherwise noted.

First published 2021

Manufactured in the United States

ISBN 9781467141925

Library of Congress Control Number: 2020944151

Notice: The information in this book is true and complete to the best of our knowledge. It is offered without guarantee on the part of the author or The History Press. The author and The History Press disclaim all liability in connection with the use of this book.

With appreciation for the storytellers who have enriched my life: Mary Grace, John Baskin, Ted Miller, Steve Hamm, Tom White, Mac Ward, Ellis Rawnsley, Eloise Rosser, Greg Hand, Jack Klumpe and Chris von Volborth.

CONTENTS

INTRODUCTION AND ACKNOWLEDGEMENTS

There is an old Siberian proverb I particularly like: "If you don't know the trees, you may be lost in the forest, but if you don't know the stories you may be lost in life." I have no idea when or where I first heard it, but it has stuck with me. Through the decades, I've found that it is the stories that make a community, bring us together and welcome strangers to the streets and neighborhoods. Every corner and building, everything we eat, every smell, every conversation, every person we see—there are stories to them all. This book tries to gather just a small part of Cincinnati's community story, its connection to books and reading.

When Fort Washington was established along the Ohio River in 1789 on the site of what is now Cincinnati, the intent was to provide a secured staging point for adventurous pioneers to settle the Northwest Territory. Fort Washington was situated opposite the Licking River on the Kentucky side of the Ohio, a small 15-acre carving from more than 300,000 acres that John Cleves Symmes purchased from the Continental Congress just a year prior to the establishment of the stockade. Though the fort was abandoned in 1803 for new quarters across the river in Newport, Kentucky, the settlers had indeed made their way to the immense rich land speculated by Symmes.

The soldiers in the fort entertained themselves as best they could in the humid summers in the Ohio Valley and the gray chill and drizzle of winter. They did this by putting on makeshift productions of dramas and comedies with which they were familiar, including a few interpretations of the Shakespeare canon, particularly *King Lear*, *Julius Caesar* and *Macbeth*, as well as *A Midsummer Night's*

Cincinnati today on the Ohio River. From the hills rising on the Kentucky side of the river, the Cincinnati skyline provides one of the most spectacular views in urban America.

Dream and *The Merry Wives of Windsor.* Granted, these homespun performances were excerpts from the plays rather than fully mounted productions, but they give an indication of what the soldiers were familiar with enough to bring with them to the frontier. And this was all decades away from the considerable bardolatry that swept America and Britain in the mid-1800s. Of course, the soldiers also brought Bibles and collections of sermons as well, those filling any moral cavities that required attention.

This literary baggage was akin to that brought by the settlers from the New England states, from the Mid-Atlantic, as well as Virginia and the Carolinas. At the beginning, the settlers were primarily Protestant, even the Irish and Germans who crossed the Atlantic and kept moving inland once they reached the shores of the United States. Their bookish possessions were few for the most part, but in addition to the Bible, there were rudimentary primers, John Bunyan's *The Pilgrim's Progress* and an almanac or two that were unpacked when they arrived.

The creation of schools in Cincinnati was not far behind. In 1791, James Lloyd, an Irish immigrant who had recently landed in the settlement, built a log cabin for a schoolhouse close to the river on what is now the end of

Sycamore Street. Schools meant instruction. Instruction meant literacy, and literacy led to a sense of the real importance of the printed word. By the end of the nineteenth century, Cincinnati's claim to education fame would rest on its production of William McGuffey's Readers (in a distant second place, perhaps, was the city's embrace of physical education in the public schools, attributable to its German immigrants and the Turner Movement).

Just two short years after Lloyd built his schoolhouse, a newspaper was established in Cincinnati. The first issue of the *Centinel of the North-Western Territory* was published by William Maxwell on November 9, 1793.[1] A native of New Jersey, Maxwell made his way to Pittsburgh and then came down the Ohio River with a printing press. Before he journeyed to Cincinnati, however, Maxwell first went to Lexington, Kentucky, where he began printing in the first days of 1793. Not endearing himself to the established newspaper already being printed in Lexington by John Bradford, the *Kentucky Gazette*, Maxwell ventured to Cincinnati and announced his intention:

> *The Printer of the* Centinel of the North-Western Territory *to the Public: Having arrived at Cincinnati, he has applied himself to that which has been the principal object of his removal to this country, the Publication of a Newspaper.*

The *Centinel* was published weekly until June 1796, when it merged with Edmund Freeman's *Freeman's Journal*. The approaching nineteenth century would see a bonanza of newspapers in Cincinnati, more than one hundred different newspapers over the course of the 1800s: English, German and Hebrew; for Republican, Whig and Democrat; serving African American, German, Irish and Jewish citizens; for the likes of Catholics, Episcopalians, Baptists, Presbyterians and Methodists. The newspapers spoke to labor unions, businessmen, consumers, temperance advocates, abolitionists and anti-abolitionists.[2] Depending on their owners and editors—and their customers—the newspapers' editorials and articles railed and ranted, cajoled, praised, exhorted, explained, lied, advocated, opposed and informed. If a reader had a cause, there was a newspaper to support it. And if a rival newspaper opposed the cause, well, someone's hash would be settled. Certainly, some of these publications seemed to go out of print almost as soon as the presses stopped rolling for the day, but there were many that lasted decades, even a century or more up to our own time. But all this journalism meant that Cincinnatians were avid (and opinionated) readers from the very beginnings of the city.

Cincinnati fast became a national center for publishing and the production of paper, type and ink. In an 1855 British publication, *Trubner's Bibliographic Guide to American Literature*, the editors noted that Cincinnati had a burgeoning business profile that revolved around the printed word.[3] With nearly 120,000 inhabitants, the city had twelve publishing houses, employing 700 workers. Many of these publishers included binders and booksellers as part of their commercial endeavors. Add to this the number of firms that cast type for the printing houses, the ink manufacturers that supplied the printers, the libraries and reading rooms and all the associated trades involved in putting a book or periodical in the hands of the reader, and by the 1880s there were hundreds of these businesses. It all became part of the city's profile of arts, culture and learning that led Cincinnati to be called the "Literary Emporium of the West." It wasn't hyperbole in the least.

When it came to literature, Cincinnati was certainly on the map. Actors and actresses touring the country had a main stop in Cincinnati in performance of the most popular plays of the age, including a great deal of Shakespeare, more about which the reader will find in the final chapter of this book. The prominent authors of the 1800s also had Cincinnati on their lecture tours—Charles Dickens, Mark Twain and Oscar Wilde, among many. Of course, as the citizens of any city would in the case of rapid settlement and business growth, Cincinnatians were quick to toot the local horn. As early as the 1820s, they were already calling their home the "Queen of the West" in their commercial boosterism, and inevitably, such sentiment makes its way into literature. The big example of this is when poet Henry Wadsworth Longfellow took pen to hand in 1857 to versify a tribute to the wine produced by Nicholas Longworth from his extensive vineyards along Cincinnati's hillsides. Full disclosure: apparently Longworth sent Longfellow a case of his Catawba sparkling wine, free of charge, and Longfellow responded in his own currency. That's the Long and the short of it. In "Catawba Wine," Longfellow waxed rhapsodic, no doubt influenced by the open bottle or two at his elbow:

This song of mine
Is a song of the Vine
To be sung by the glowing embers
Of wayside inns,
When the rain begins
To darken the drear Novembers.

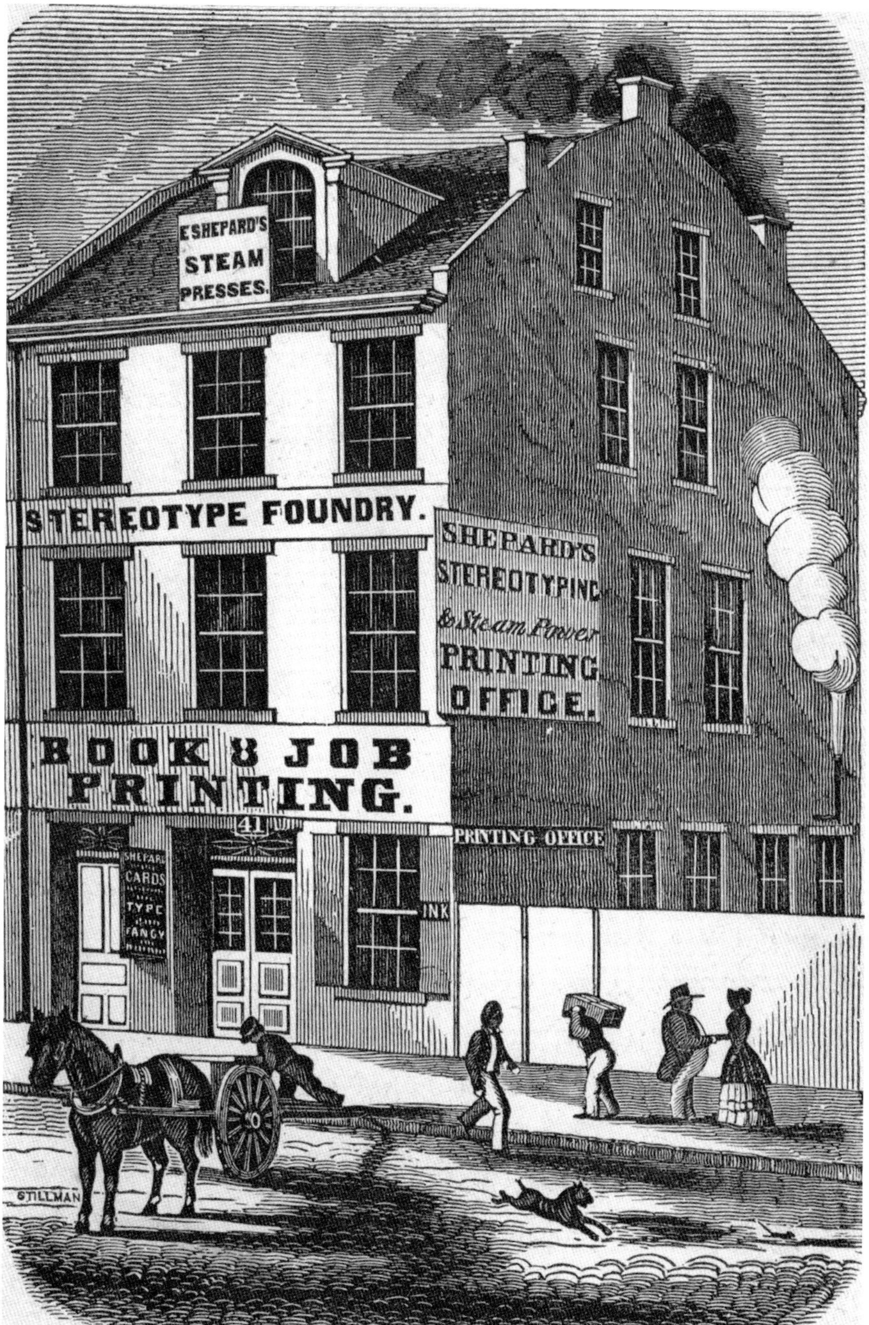

One of Cincinnati's many printers and publishers in the mid-nineteenth century, Shepard's printing business and type foundry was typical of the enormous growth of the book industry in nineteenth-century Cincinnati.

(Well, certainly nothing has changed about Cincinnati weather since then.) The poem continues for ten more stanzas about this wine and that and how they fail in comparison with Longworth's vintages. It concludes:

And this Song of the Vine,
This greeting of mine,
The winds and the birds shall deliver
To the Queen of the West,
In her garlands dressed,
On the banks of the Beautiful River.

Sadly, as important as Nicholas Longworth was in furthering an American wine industry, his Catawba grapes did not last long in Cincinnati, mainly because of a powdery mildew that wiped out his vineyards. But there is still Longfellow's verse; though it borders on doggerel (and I believe there is considerable charm, if not lasting merit, to doggerel), it continues to be embraced as a cousin in Cincinnati's literary lineage. And even as the local book industries were changing with the approach of the twentieth century, they remained strong, and the "Queen of the West" was still a popular poetic trope, even to the extent of using it on the penny postcard:

A Toast to Cincinnati

Here's to Old Cincy, the Queen of the West!
A soot-begrimed city, but still nobly blest;
For it's here that fine arts with the frivolous twine,
A veritable Deutschland just over the Rhine.
Her beautiful hilltops, and sweet girls the hit,
The dust that we breathe, productive of grit;
Her theatres, Dutch lunches, resorts and the Zoo,
Skyscrapers, the tumult, and the spirit to "do."
The kindliest greeting from all whom we meet,
A good draught of beer every ten or twelve feet;
So let's drink to the shades of the good and the bad,
And never forget the fine time we have had.

This postcard poem was written by James K. Stewart of the "Arcade" in Cincinnati and was sent in 1910 from "Bill" to "George," Bill telling George that he was meeting a crowd of their friends, presumably to wash down the city dust with a beer or two. A city that embraces poetry and beer can't be all bad, and another boosterism postcard printed in 1907 is evidence of that:

> *Were you ever in Cincinnati, Ohio?*
> *Where they brew good beer and are never slow,*
> *Where the drinking bars are certainly stars*
> *And are known the world over—even in Mars,*
> *But space don't permit of telling half,*
> *Just come over soon and—it is to laugh,*
> *And when you reach here we'll kill the fatted calf.*

The postcard is illustrated with a pretty woman behind a parasol with doves on her head; there is a peacock at the top of the poem, and at the bottom are cigars, beer and rye and glasses for both. You know, a shot and a beer and smoke 'em if you got 'em. Now who wouldn't want to come to Cincinnati, work diligently on improving the poetic form and tip a glass or two?

My own visit to Cincinnati that was a first brush with its literary heritage came by happenstance in 1972, and I was, in fact, a stranger to the city. Growing up in Phillipsburg, a little farm town north of Dayton, I came to Cincinnati occasionally with my family to see a ballgame or visit the zoo, but that was it. I had never explored the city and I knew nothing about it except the smells of factories along the highway as you headed downtown toward the river. Then, when I was an undergraduate at Wright State University, one spring afternoon I drove down I-75 with some friends to see a Reds game. And while it was a great time in history to watch the Big Red Machine at Riverfront Stadium in the 1970s, the game was the least part of the story of that particular day. It is because I visited a legendary bookstore, and I credit my friend Steve Hamm, who decided we would go to Cincinnati. Steve was a fellow anthropology major at Wright State, but his life experience was mountains and miles in the distance from mine. A few years older than me, Steve was originally a small-towner as well, from Minnesota, but he had driven cross-country when he was a teenager, served in the navy during the Vietnam War and set anchor in the various ports of Asia. After his service, Steve went to Mexico for a couple of college years, taking time to travel around and about the country. When he enrolled at Wright State and I met him, the "experiential learning" aspect of my education began.

Arriving in Cincinnati that day, Steve made our first stop at 633 Main Street, the three-story home of Acres of Books. I'll write more of the bookstore in this volume, but for now the story is of that day in 1972. When

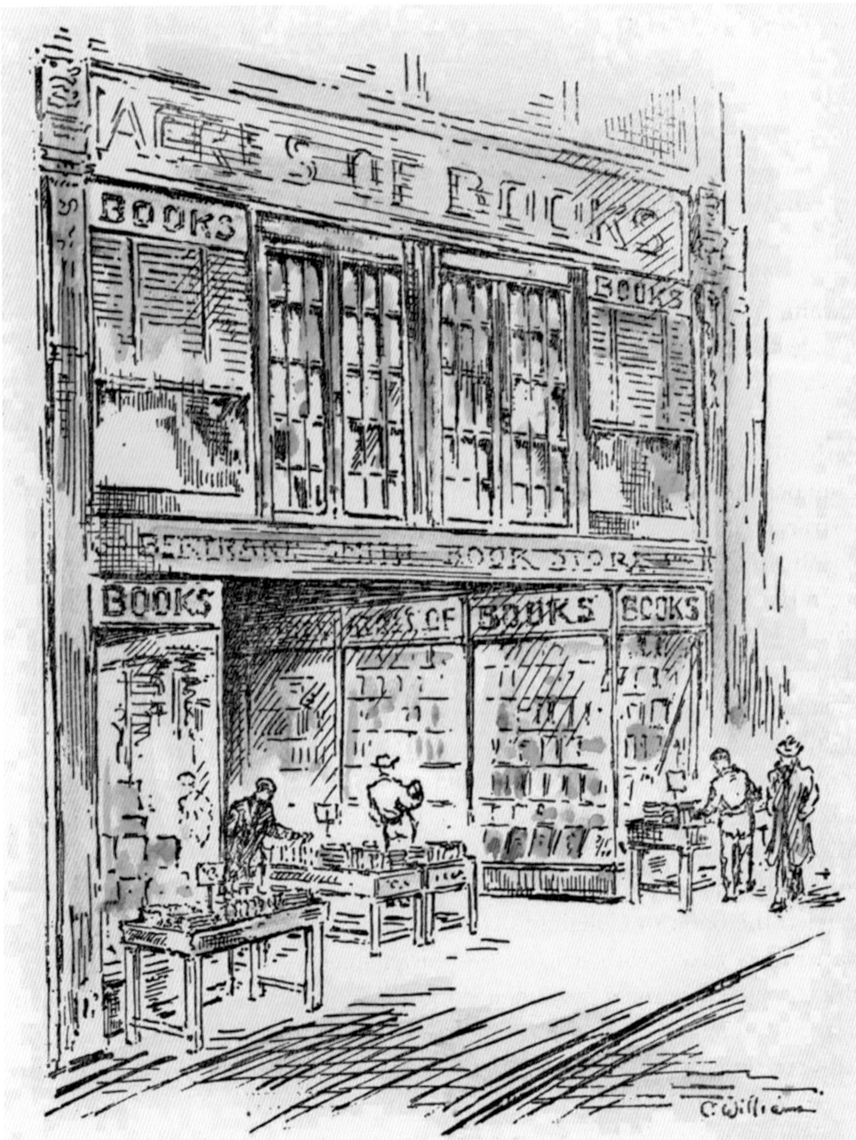

The legendary Acres of Books on Main Street, circa 1950. The great bookman Bertrand Smith founded the store, and his legacy was carried on by his son Bertrand Jr. and John Coleman. *Watercolor by Caroline Williams.*

we walked through the door, I thought I was in a wonderland. Growing up, I had the public libraries, Wilkie's in downtown Dayton and the Walden's Bookstore in the mall, but this was something else entirely, a palace of books. There were three floors of used and out-of-print volumes, and it was like I was seeing all the world's Christmas presents unwrapped and on display. It was dim and dusty and slightly decrepit in the best of ways. Hanging on the walls were various historical prints and etchings, as well as photographs and period engravings of notable authors like William Shakespeare and Mark Twain, Walt Whitman and Thomas Mann, Jonathan Swift and F. Scott Fitzgerald. I wish I had paid more attention to all of that at the time because it wasn't long ago that I acquired one of those photos. And I have no idea who it is. I queried both friends and strangers who might have an idea of this early twentieth-century figure with spectacles and long gray hair and a long gray beard. Not Tolstoy, not Whitman, not anyone we can identify. Still, it's a striking photograph, and I treasure it as a remnant of a great bookstore.

John Coleman was the proprietor at that time, having bought the store from Bertram Smith Jr., son of the founder, Smith Sr., and he ruled it like the true bookman he was—somewhat taciturn and very knowledgeable about the good stock. So Steve and I wandered the floors and the shelves. I found the anthropology/social sciences/whatever else section and prised from the tightly packed books what I thought was a treasure and what seems now as an incredibly obscure book, Polish anthropologist Bronisław Malinowski's 1922 study *Argonauts of the Western Pacific*, his monograph on New Guinea. Malinowski was one of the giants of twentieth-century ethnographers and frequently mentioned by my anthropology professor AKM Aminul Islam. I carried the book to Coleman's counter and watched him wrap it in brown paper and bind it with string. I had never made such a beautiful purchase. But a couple of weeks later, when Professor Islam learned I had this book, he fiercely negotiated a trade. At the time, I thought I wanted a beat-up Leica camera more than a turgid academic tome. I probably still do. But Professor Islam and I never really got along after that.

From Acres of Books, Steve drove us over to Walnut Street for an early dinner at Grammer's, of course lamented now in its empty and distressed state but vibrant and colorful back then. You see, Steve Hamm has always been this Falstaffian figure of a man who explores the world through its food and drink, music and photography (and accommodating me, occasionally books). Our wives are very tolerant, I suppose. From my undergrad days of long hair and long nights of reading and talking, I have gone bald and gray where what little hair remains, but the long nights of reading remain, if broken up sometimes with a quick nap in the early evening. Steve's immense red Viking beard he had in those days has gone to a trimmed silver now, but the eye twinkle is still there, generally indicating he is in the vicinity of good wine, an interesting character on the sidewalk, a plate of good food or a pretty woman. At Grammer's we had beer and sausages and spaetzle and plenty of all of it. I suppose we went to the Reds game, but I have no memory of that, just of that wonderful bookstore and a fine meal—and these days I seem to remember more occasions of good food and good stories than anything else. Even today, I feel that on that particular afternoon, I began to hear Cincinnati's tales from the streets and people around me.

Today there is a vibrant writing community in Cincinnati that is matched with exceptional libraries and literacy programs, book arts, buildings and some very fine bookstores selling both used and new volumes. All of this contributes to the heritage of Cincinnatians authoring, printing, buying, reading and treasuring books. Of course many local bookstores have disappeared over the past decades, like Acres of Books, Kidd's, Lance's, New World Bookshop, Significant Books, the Dust Jacket, Fountain Square Books, Robert Clarke's bookstore as part of his publishing business, U.P. James, Stewart & Kidd, Crazy Ladies Bookstore and even the local franchises of the national chains like Little Professor, Border's, Walden's and some of the locations for Half Price Books and Barnes & Noble. There are many more, which is not surprising when we consider the dozens and dozens that have been a part of Cincinnati's history since the beginning of the 1800s. We have some great ones today in the Cincinnati area: Ohio Bookstore, Downbound Books, Smith & Hannon, Joseph-Beth, Roebling Books & Coffee, Duttenhofer's, Homestead, Iris Book Café, Blue Manatee, Commonwealth Books, Cincy Book Bus, Book Rack, Mulberry Street Books and Maverick's Comics, among several others.

It's the same everywhere in America and around the globe. But it's a waste of time and energy to overromanticize the passing of some bookshops and lament their demise. There's too much worthy of celebration now. However, we can and do celebrate the past. Two of the best books that have done just that are Walter Sutton's masterful *The Western Book Trade: Cincinnati as a 19th Century Publishing & Book-Trade Center*, published in 1961, and Dale Patrick Brown's witty and insightful 2011 text, *Literary Cincinnati: The Missing Chapter.* Sutton provides a vivid history of the booksellers and printers that enriched Cincinnati, and he writes of the decline of the book production trade as well. Brown tells of such figures as Alice and Phoebe Cary, Cincinnati's poet sisters; of Harriet Beecher Stowe, George Elliston and Lafcadio Hearn;

The Friends of the Public Library warehouse in the Hartwell neighborhood attracts thousands of book lovers to its annual sales and operates a regular bookstore.

and institutions like the Literary Club and the Mercantile Library. I have depended on both of these works for inspiration because of the stories they tell of a very special city and its books, and I hope I have added another perspective to this heritage with new stories of the past and of the present. Citations for both Brown and Sutton may be found in the section "Fifty Essential Books for Understanding Cincinnati."

Of course, readers and book lovers face challenges to their passions from time to time, sometimes through spasms of censorship from governments, school boards and citizen groups; sometimes through the strictures of state and local tax bases and the dips of economies; and sometimes through an unforeseen force. In the 2020 global pandemic, communities in the United States witnessed the closing of libraries and bookstores, greatly reducing access to books and reading for a large portion of the population. We developed ways around this: those of us who could afford them ordered books from online retailers, we purchased or checked out e-books or we listened to audiobooks. And in Cincinnati, we had the Cincy Book Bus, the Blue Manatee Bookstore and Literacy Project, the Literacy Network of Greater Cincinnati, Adopt a Book and other organizations that made sure books were still distributed to disadvantaged readers. Little Free Libraries continued to grow in the neighborhoods. The Friends of the Public Library launched a pop-up pandemic bookshop, and we took advantage of social media with WordPlay, Cincinnati Poetry Slam, Poetry Night at Sitwell's Coffeehouse and the Mercantile Library among many others keeping local literature alive.

Many, many people have contributed over the years to my teaching and research in books and reading, and I thank them: Jason Autry, Ludmila Gruszewska Blaim, Debbie Brawn, Colleen Brennan, Gabe Brown, Neil Choudhury, Jim Cummins, Megan Dunlevy, Billie Dziech, Bob Flischel, Dan Gottlieb, Justin Green, Terry Grundy, Savannah Gulick, Marcy Hawley, Sarah Hawley, Randi Heming, Chris Hoover, Tyler Morrison Keller, Pat Kiernan, Lauren Kirgis, Ben Kline, Gabby Kraemer, Diane Mallstrom, Yu Mao, Lisa Mauch, John McNay, Raj Mehta, Kent Meloy, Anil Menon, Onnie Middendorf, Martin Molony, Victoria Montavon, Remy Nering, Buck Niehoff, Sophia Ortiz, Mike Perrino, Brian Powers, Natalie Prager, Holly Prochaska, M.B. Reilly, Sue Reller, Cedric Rose, Jeff Ruetsche, Melissa Schirmer, Robin Selzer, Christopher Smith, Sarah Stoner, Andy Sweeny, Eira Tansey, Don Heinrich Tolzmann, Carol Tyler, Pat Van Skaik, Lisa Sweasy and the Vent Haven Museum, Sydney Vollmer, Gary Walton, Xuemao Wang, Moriah Weese, Molly Wellman, Leah Wickett, Dann Woellert, Jenny Wohlfarth, Tricia Yee and Jay Yocis. For those I've missed calling out by name, I apologize but please know that I appreciate all of you.

A view of Cincinnati and the Ohio River in 1810. Settlers arrived by flatboat, and later traveling theater companies journeyed by flatboat to perform Shakespeare plays and popular comedies and melodramas.

Thanks to my editor, John Rodrigue, for his extraordinary patience, and to my family: Joan, Josh, Sean, Courtney, Bonnie, Lily, Zo, Paul, Bobby, Arden and Honora. And thanks to all the great students I've learned from over time and who traveled to various parts of the world with me. A very special acknowledgement is due Mike Martini, with whom I was privileged to partner on *The Book Show* on WMKV-FM for three years.

A couple of years ago, I asked the noted Cincinnati graphic novelist and sign painter Justin Green to make a small wooden sign for me. On it, I wanted a phrase I use as a way sign in my teaching and in my own walking about the world. Justin came up with a beautiful design of red, gold, blue and green and a book with these words floating from the pages: *And here begins a tale…*

1

MAKING BOOKS AND PUTTING THEM IN THE HANDS OF READERS

The creation of a book begins with a community need, a necessity that defines a gathering of people who interact with one another on a daily basis who need information, inspiration, solace, emotion and entertainment. A book in a community fills that need because it spurs readers to action, or anger, or laughter or curiosity. And the making of a book is not complete when it is in the hands of a reader or, in fact, when a reader is finished with it. That's because a book is never completely made or created. The process goes on and on until the human memory of it is gone. A book is a great many things that rise and come together, from the author to the reader. And then to the next reader, and the next and the next. In the beginning—and what a magic phrase that is—in the beginning, many of these functions, these exercises in art and craft, may have been accomplished by the same person. Even today, in an artisan environment, maybe *all* of these endeavors could be undertaken by the same person.

After the initial reader, a book lives on. On the high western façade of Carl Blegen Library at the University of Cincinnati are these words from poet John Milton: "For books are not absolutely dead things but do contain a potencie of life in them to be as active as those whose progeny they are." It's a fairly close paraphrase of Milton's *Areopagitica; A Speech of Mr. John Milton For the Liberty of Unlicenc'd Printing, To the Parliament of England*, written in 1644 during the English Civil War in protest against censorship.[4] The phrase is carved in limestone, present there since this Cincinnati library opened in 1930, and since it is just a bit changed from Milton's original

Tools of the trade in the Preservation Lab at the University of Cincinnati's Walter C. Langsam Library. The lab is a cooperative program for book preservation and conservation between UC and the Public Library of Cincinnati and Hamilton County. Employed by both institutions, its staff does extraordinary restoration work and repair on rare books and materials, as well as important circulating collections.

prose, the meaning can be changed a bit as well to become meaningful to us. John Milton was saying that once created, books have a life beyond their authors, that they take on lives of their own when they are read and passed on. Their potency is real. A book becomes part of a community. When it is passed from hand to hand, from citizen to citizen, reading becomes part of a community.

But it starts somewhere. That phrase "In the beginning" is as captivating to the mind as "Once upon a time." They both signal a point of creation, and in Cincinnati, that creation came with establishment of printing and ink enterprises. The books the early Cincinnati settlers carried with them were, perhaps, just an impetus for those citizens to create more when they got here. To be a community of any substance, the city had to educate and empower its residents in whatever endeavors they chose to undertake. The manufacture of ink and type, the building of printing presses, the printing and publishing of books and the establishment of schools and libraries made Cincinnati a community. By 1825, the Cincinnati Steam Paper Mill had been established, and it was followed the next year by the operation of the Cincinnati Type Foundry, which for decades afterward would issue a type specimen book that was subscribed to by printing firms around the country.

In the beginning and once upon a time, there were printers and publishers in Cincinnati. Quite a number of them. In fact, by the 1830s, Cincinnati was unquestionably the book center of the West, that stretch of America beyond the Appalachian Mountains. At that time in the United States, only Boston, New York and Philadelphia surpassed Cincinnati in book production. More than 350,000 books were printed, bound and published in the city, and a decade later, almost 2 million were published. William Holmes McGuffey and his readers seemed to take over the schoolrooms of America. McGuffey was an interesting sort. Miami University pays tribute to him with a statue and small museum, honoring his tenure there as a professor from 1826 to 1836 and as the place where he began to write the textbooks that carried his name into history. There is a legend, though,

In addition to printing, design, publishing and paper manufacturing, the city's immense book-oriented businesses also included several ink factories. Billing itself as "The Oldest and Largest Printing Ink Works in the West," the Queen City Printing Ink Company was founded in 1860 by John Rychen and George DeGolyer. With offices in four other cities—Chicago, Philadelphia, Denver and New York—the home Cincinnati factory was located at 600 West Fifth Street.

that when he left Oxford, Ohio, to become the president of Cincinnati College, he advised parents not to send their sons to Miami as they would inevitably become drunkards. Whether that is true or not, McGuffey was stepping into a similar academic world in Cincinnati. Cincinnati College was founded in 1819, and by the time it fully merged with the University of Cincinnati in 1918, the only vestige of it was its law school, which had previously merged with UC in 1897—all of which is a whopperjawed way of the University of Cincinnati claiming a founding date of 1819. All of those confusing chronologies aside, the Reverend McGuffey (yes, he was an ordained Presbyterian minister) had a way about him when it came to speechifying and lecturing. Besides his Cincinnati-based aspersion on Miami University, the other tale told of him is that his lectures on moral philosophy were so popular that the designated lecture room was always packed and that in a room above, holes were drilled in the floor so that those sequestered there could hear the goings-on below them.

He was a singular presence in the classroom, but in his world of writing and publishing his textbooks, McGuffey enlisted the help of his brother Alexander and Catherine Beecher, sister of Harriet Beecher Stowe and quite a force in her own right on the issue of women's education. By the time the readers were being published by the American Book Company in Cincinnati, the sales were in the tens of millions.[5] Of course, textbooks accounted for the lion's share of this part of the book world, but there was much more to Cincinnati as a literary powerhouse than the books themselves. In the 1800s, Cincinnati also supplied paper, type specimens and ink to the nation. Of no small account in the nineteenth century was ink. And the most notable ink factory in Cincinnati was one that became known around the world.

Levi Addison Ault was born in Canada and came to Cincinnati in 1876; there he found work in a company that manufactured lampblack and rosins. He worked his way up to become its top salesman, and dealing in lampblack, Ault had an idea that he could make a good ink business with it. A young man who worked for him, Frank Wiborg, invested $10,000 to become an equal partner in Ault & Wiborg, the partnership the two of them formed in 1878. And over the next half century, as color printing and lithography developed in the mainstream of magazine and book production, the Ault & Wiborg inks gained an international reputation. The sumptuous colors in its printing inks and dyes were highly esteemed, bolstered by the company motto, *Hic et Ubique*, or "here and everywhere," and its series of poster ads showing off its color offerings became prized works of art. Issued on a regular basis before gathered into one publication, the advertisements of

William Holmes McGuffey, erstwhile professor of Miami University and president of Cincinnati College, was the creator of the McGuffey Readers, the most popular textbooks of the nineteenth century. Millions of copies were sold throughout the country, and on some of his readers and spellers, he was assisted by his brother Alexander and Catherine Beecher, the sister of Harriet Beecher Stowe and a prominent advocate for women's education. Though she had no personal connection to the University of Cincinnati, a women's building constructed on the campus in 1915 was named for her.

Ault & Wiborg exhibited the work of noted designers and bookmen. With a variety of themes, typography designs and specific colors, the small posters easily promoted the quality of the inks. By the end of World War I, Ault & Wiborg was the leading producer of lithography and printing inks in the world. However, as the 1920s edged along toward the Great Depression, the company was changing. Both Wiborg and Ault died in 1930. Two years earlier, Ault sold his share in the company and retired. His name lives on in Cincinnati through Ault Park. Levi Ault was an amateur naturalist, and he fell in love with the local parks and served on the Cincinnati Parks Board for two decades. He donated 204 acres to the city to create Ault Park, still a showplace in the city.

If there are books and magazines, you need somewhere to put them, and another Cincinnati company certainly helped fill the shelves—by building them. The Globe-Wernicke Company formed in 1899 with the merger of Cincinnati's Globe Files Company, established in 1882, and a Minneapolis firm, the Wernicke Company, which opened in 1893. Before their merger,

With the merging of several publishers, Cincinnati's American Book Company became the publisher of the McGuffey Readers. Its building on Pike Street is now luxury apartments, but there are historical photos in the lobby and, beneath an entry rug, the tiled logo of this famous publisher.

Globe made filing cabinets and desks, and Wernike made bookcases. The combined company became a world leader in office furniture, with factories in five countries. Locally, Globe-Wernicke in Norwood, the small city encircled by Cincinnati, contributed heavily to the established book culture of the Queen City until the factory closed in 1964. But if you are of a certain age, a certain generation, you remember library card catalogues, filing shelves, card catalogue boxes, file trays and any number of Globe-Wernicke products. If it was in a library and made of mahogany or walnut or oak, the odds are good that it was made by Globe-Wernicke.

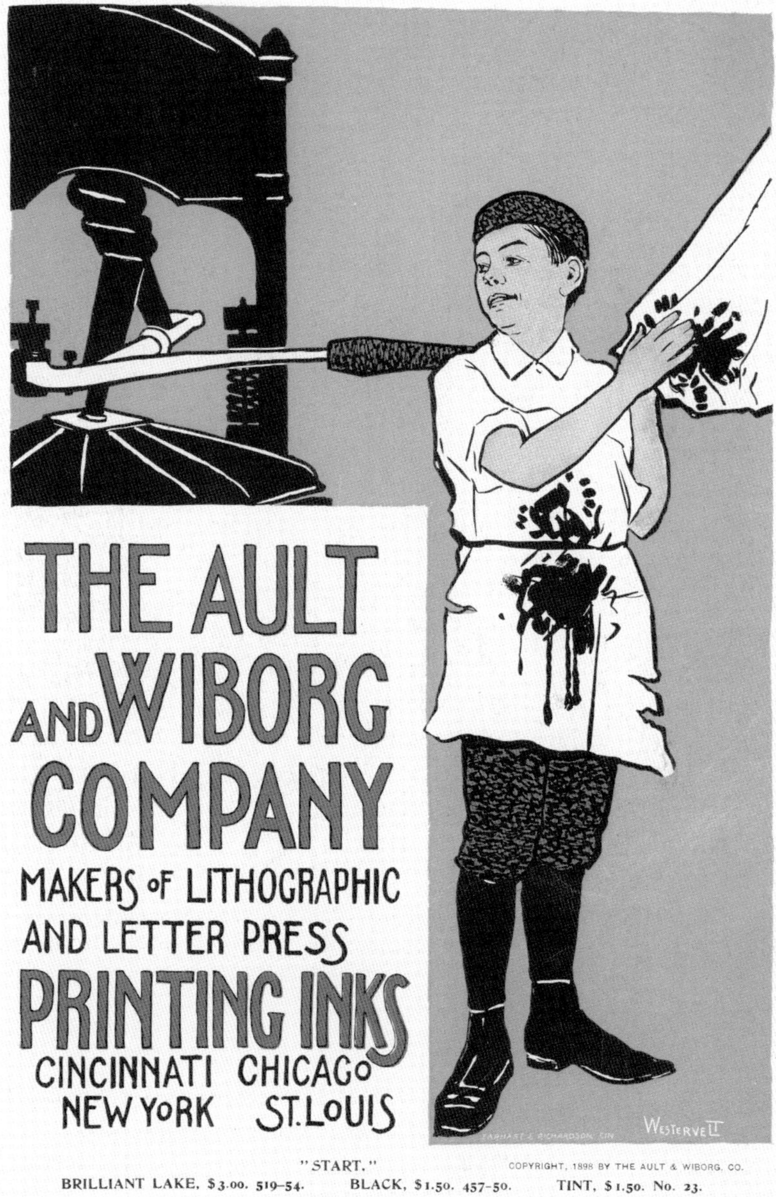

Another venerable Cincinnati ink company, and one with a global reach, was the Ault & Wiborg firm, founded in 1878 by Levi Addison Ault and Frank Wiborg. Their company became the world's largest manufacturer of printing inks and lithograph supplies. Ault & Wiborg's advertisements for such industry publications as the *Inland Printer* were commissioned works from some of the country's best graphic artists and they rapidly became highly sought for collectibles.

The signature product, though, and one greatly prized today is Globe-Wernicke's "elastic bookcase" or, as it is more popularly known, the barrister bookcase. These modular units were built so that sections of shelves, each one a box of sorts with a sliding glass door covering it, could be stacked together. The carpentry work in building these units was of a very high standard, with the most popular finishes in a golden oak or rich reddish mahogany. The company had a strong advertising presence for its library products, regularly issuing ads that provided an attached bookmark or a premium for ordering books. But by World War II, much of the Globe-Wernicke's facilities were converted for military production, and a series of mergers and takeovers doomed the Cincinnati company's library heritage. In the 1960s, production moved out of Norwood. The factory land was sold, and the buildings were demolished for redevelopment. What remains in Cincinnati are some beautiful vintage bookcases and cabinets and the legendary name that built them.

These firms were part of the much larger picture of print and publishing in the city. There were many lithographers, from the Young & Klein firm to the multinational giant Strobridge Lithography Company, which dominated the production of theater and circus posters. After entering business in 1854 with a partnership in a small company that printed and sold stationery, Hines Strobridge eventually established his own enterprise, building a factory along the Miami-Erie Canal in 1884. He hired lithographers and designers to create the posters and book illustrations and, with the many other printing and lithography companies, competed with colorful and ornate advertisements in the city's annual directories. The city was alive with the slamming din of printing presses and the casting of type. As part of the local industries that helped form and sustain it, the Ohio Mechanics Institute developed a lithography and printing curriculum, training the workforce for the trades. Then it all seemed to disappear and be forgotten. After World War II, the Cincinnati printing business was greatly diminished when the larger firms were acquired in mergers, causing the local heritage of Cincinnati printing and publishing to sink almost into oblivion.

That heritage has been revived. In 2016, Gary Walton, a retired professor at Cincinnati State Technical and Community College, created the Cincinnati Type & Print Museum in Lower Price Hill on the city's west side. Walton, a printer himself who taught graphic arts for four decades, gathered printing presses, type cases and everything needed for the trade into a small building that celebrates Cincinnati's rich history with the written word. It is a working museum, with Walton and his assistant director Jacob Simpson teaching the

Early advertising for the Strobridge Lithography Company, which would grow into one of the world's largest printers of circus and show posters.

A lithography classroom at the Ohio Mechanics Institute/Ohio College of Applied Science, circa 1910. The school was founded in 1828 with the purpose of training young men in the manufacturing trades of the city. Because of its standing as preeminent center for printing and publishing, Cincinnati had a great need for skilled craftsmen in the printing arts.

craft of letterpress printing to those neighborhood citizens struggling with poverty in order to get them into the workforce. The museum is another keystone in commemorating the local printing industry.

So the books are written, they're designed, printed and bound. Now, to get them in the hands of readers. With the McGuffey Readers, it was rather straightforward: sell them to schools. Put them in classrooms. Sometimes those schoolrooms were packed with children in antiquated buildings or in airy, newly funded structures. Sometimes, depending on health needs and educational philosophy, they were outdoors in the fresh air. But those were schoolbooks. For the general reader, there were bookstores.

It is said that the legendary Acres of Books had its beginning in the 1920s from the bar of a Cincinnati saloon. Several years past his service in World War I, Bertram Smith Sr., the iconoclastic founder of the bookstore, sold used and rare books from his perch on a stool, presumably with a drink

Exhibited at the Type & Print Museum are type cases and building plaques of Cincinnati's early printers and lithographers.

at his elbow. He knew his stuff, and as business picked up, he scrounged about and found the wherewithal to open a store on Main Street in 1927. As the story goes—and who knows all the particulars so many decades later—Smith decided he had enough of Cincinnati and his marriage so he gave the store over to his wife in 1934 and headed for the West Coast, opening another Acres of Books in Long Beach, California, where it thrived for over seventy years. By and by, the Cincinnati store was operated by Bertram Jr., who became a legend himself and one of the most knowledgeable sorts in the country when it came to the rare book trade. His store was a treasure house, and this younger Smith frequently sold or gave important books to

Children reading their textbooks in an open-air classroom at Dyer School, 1913. The Open-Air School Movement was an educational concept first developed in Germany in 1904, and given its strong Germanic heritage and education philosophy, it was not surprising that Cincinnati quickly adopted this method of teaching, and many other cities did as well. Holding classes in the fresh air was mainly an urban response to health problems of the inner-city poor. Overcrowded and stuffy classrooms were believed to contribute to airborne illnesses.

Children in the tubercular sanitarium read their books in the fresh outdoors, 1913. The prevalence of tuberculosis and its spread among children was a driving factor in outdoor education.

A bookshop storefront on Main Street, 1930. The store also served as a storage facility for the public library.

local libraries, always with his little red or green bookshop stamp pasted on an endpaper. The stamp was an image of a book with "Bertram Smith's Acres of Books. Cincinnati" printed on it. Inside, the wooden stairs led from floor to floor, with old engravings and photographs along the way. The aquatints and watercolors were of pastoral scenes and cities, the prints often taken from books that were falling apart to the point of no rescue. The photographs? Most of them were of authors dead and gone—Mark Twain, Leo Tolstoy, William Butler Yeats, Booth Tarkington and others—with the occasional image of an unidentified reader joining their company. The common ones were for sale, and for the rare or unusual ones, if you were a favored customer or had the right kind of bibliophile look about you, those could be purchased as well. In 1970, Smith retired and sold the store to his longtime employee John Coleman, a fine bookman in his own right.

There was a definite scent to older books in the store, as there is in any used bookshop worthy of the name, and it is much more than the scientific determination that organic components like wood pulp and cellulose are reacting with heat and light. In hard terms, it is decay but in the way a book lover inhales it, the smell is both wistful desire and soft comfort. That was the smell in Acres of Books. In that, it is best just to allow for the romance to take hold because in used books, there are the unknown stories of the human hands that once held it or the human spirit that read the words. And every once in a while, those stories of previous owners are revealed with a presentation note on the endpaper, scribbled marginalia on the pages or a bookmark that was once a business card, a wildflower or recipe. The books remain as alive as the original owner once was.

Just up Main and across the street another great Cincinnati bookstore was established, the Ohio Book Store, a Cincinnati institution to this day. Established by James Hardwick in 1940, just a few years after Smith's shop, the Ohio Book Store moved in 1961 but remained on Main Street. A beautiful building with a terra-cotta frontage, it was constructed in 1916 as an investment property for the University of Cincinnati (you can still see the university seal with UC's true founding date of 1870 on the façade). It is distinguished by the store's green awning, and unlike the standard image of a bookstore selling the used, out of print and rare, the store is bright and airy. There are five floors of books, bins of vintage magazines and beautiful first editions in glass-fronted cabinets. Proprietor James Fallon began working for Hardwick in 1956 and bought the store from him in 1971. After Acres of Books finally locked its door and shuttered its windows in 1991, Fallon bought some of its stock and continued the tradition of great Cincinnati bookshops.

While there is always some measure of truth to the matter, for all the fuss and folderol about Cincinnati as a conservative burg, there have been some extraordinary counters to that sentiment when it comes to books and reading. Certainly, the politicians and law enforcement had their day, the most prominent of whom was Simon Leis, who worked variously as a Hamilton County prosecutor, a judge in the court of common pleas and as the sheriff of Hamilton County. One of the indelible images of him is the photo of his

A Cincinnati institution, the venerable Ohio Bookstore on Main Street.

Hamilton County prosecutors raid the Queen City News in suburban Blue Ash, looking to root out pornography, 1972. The pornography wars raged in Cincinnati for the better part of three decades, with bookstores and newsstands being periodically raided and closed down by the sheriff's office as Cincinnatians debated what they did and did not want as reading material in their community. *Photo by Jack Klumpe.*

staff forcing entry into the Queen City News wholesaler in Blue Ash, intent on seizing pornography and prosecuting the owners. Pornography aside—and what exactly constituted something pornographic—Leis may or may not have known exactly what he liked, but he most certainly knew what he didn't like and that was anything that smacked of the counterculture. One of the most noteworthy manifestations of changing social awareness at that time was the Crazy Ladies Bookstore in Northside. Founded in 1979 by Carolyn Dellenbach, the feminist bookshop honored all the women who went their own way, despite any obstacles put in their path by the rest of the world. Crazy Ladies became a community center for gay and lesbian books and programming with lectures on spirituality and feminism. The store closed as a retail bookstore in 2002 but kept its purpose of social action alive through the creation of the Greater Cincinnati Women's Resource Center and the

Melanie Moore's wonderful Book Bus, a pop-up bookshop on wheels that frequents cafés, flea markets and festivals. Moore uses the profits from her modern-day *Parnassus on Wheels* to purchase children's books for distribution to Cincinnati-area elementary schools and recreation centers.

housing of the Ohio Lesbian Archives, created in 1989 by Phebe Beiser and Victoria Ramstetter. Eventually, the Northside center closed completely in 2006, and the Archives moved to the Clifton United Methodist Church.

Covering the distance between books and readers is eased with the establishment of bookstores and libraries, but it can be closed considerably through mobility as well with the use of such things as bookmobiles, Little Free Libraries and literacy services. The aim is to get the books to the people in any way possible. And if the readers are young, literacy programs fostered by the likes of the Blue Manatee Bookstore with its innovative endeavors like virtual storytelling and the provision of books to disadvantaged children, as well as similar efforts by the Literacy Network of Greater Cincinnati, fulfill that social contract. The Princeton City Schools in the northern reaches of Cincinnati has the Mobile Book Center, a bus that travels the school district, providing books and technology to families and students who do not have easy access to a library. And then there is the Cincy Book Bus. It was established in 2019 with a 1962 mint-green Volkswagon Transporter van by retired English teacher Melanie Moore, inspired by Christopher Morley's 1915 classic *Parnassus on Wheels* about an itinerant bookseller who drives his horse and wagon from town to town.[6] Moore's bus is also a bookshop on wheels she parks outside coffee shops, farmers markets and neighborhood festivals to sell her stock of classics, special editions and popular fiction. The sides are rolled up, and the store is open. It is essentially a pop-up bookshop, with profits from the sales used to buy children's books for schools, recreation centers and women's shelters.

2

CLUBS AND COLLECTORS

In 1819, when Cincinnati College was founded, a set of rules and regulations was printed and distributed to the students and faculty.[7] Besides the typical regulations about academic life and curricula requirements, there were also rules that were mainly proscriptions on behavior: "Any student convicted of sending or receiving a challenge to fight a duel, or who shall carry such challenge, or be a second in a duel, or any wise aid or abet it, shall be expelled from the college." Another rule forbade students from going to a "tavern or tipling house" without the permission of a faculty member. Presumably these rules were created because there was real need for them.

There was also a rule about reading material: "No student shall possess or read any indecent, impious, or irreligious books; and if any student shall be convicted thereof, he shall be punished according to the nature and heinousness of the offence, by admonition, public reprehension, dismission, or expulsion, from College." It was the duty of the college officers to visit the boardinghouses and rooms of the students to make sure there were no scandalous books about or "spirituous or fermented liquors" squirreled away. The college had a small library of sorts, but apparently it did not contain all the sorts of books the students wished to read. On top of the prohibitions against caches of booze and books, the students were not permitted to insult their fellows upon pain of punishment from the faculty. And so, amid all this, the Philomathic Society was born, actually organizing in 1818 before the college opened its doors. It had the typical lofty aims of a literary society, that is, create a small library for itself, do some public good (the members planted some trees) and write flowery essays and poetry. It would publish a literary magazine filled with historical articles, poetry and literary essays.

The Cincinnati College rules seemed meant for them, however. The Philomathic members had a rival literary society at the college, the Erophebic Society, and as the years went by, some antagonism developed between the two.[8] Vulgarities were exchanged when rival members met with each other, engaging in what could only be called immoral language, and in one incident when the Philomathics and Erophebics were embroiled in a verbal literary contest, a fight broke out between one George Wilson of Philos and William Lytle of the Erops. The attending faculty members stepped between them, and while there is no record of who had the advantage, Lytle might have emerged the winner, supposed only in that he had the moxie. Lytle became a valiant general during the Civil War, wounded more than once and eventually killed in battle; he was nationally celebrated for his poetry. His sword equaled the might of his pen.

And that Wilson fellow was a troublemaker, once chastised for talking during a Philomathics meeting and then responding that he was only asking a fellow member to "go whoring with him." His crassness was decidedly considered unliterary at the time, and it resulted in the society's president fining him a dollar. If the society had a swear jar, undoubtedly it was well filled.

The Cincinnati College literary societies were an indication of the growing number of book clubs and societies in Cincinnati. The most well-known club, and one that continues today, is the Semi-Colon Club, formed around 1829.[9] Its members were some of the most influential citizens in the community, including Samuel P. Chase, Nathan Guilford, Daniel Drake, Lyman Beecher, Elizabeth Blackwell, Catherine Beecher and her sister Harriet Beecher Stowe. It was a mixed-gender club, which was unusual for the age. Members gave readings of their literary efforts and discussed recent books and current affairs. Today, the Semi-Colon Club meets at the Harriet Beecher Stowe House on Gilbert Avenue and continues its tradition of lectures and discussions on contemporary issues in Cincinnati.

Interests in literature and the building of libraries, both personal and public, fostered a number of Cincinnati book collectors, one of whom was Enoch Terry Carson. Back in 1895, William A. Procter, namesake of his father and the cofounder of Procter & Gamble, served on the University of Cincinnati's board of directors (as the members were known then when UC was a municipal institution). As a gesture of his concern for the university's academic advancement, he purchased three private libraries as a gift to UC,

William A. Procter, son of the cofounder of the Procter & Gamble Company, served on the University of Cincinnati's board of directors from 1899 to 1906. He purchased three extraordinary private libraries in the city on Shakespeare, chemistry and history and exploration and presented them to the university as its library's founding collections.

the chemical library of Timothy Norton, the Americana and global travel and exploration volumes that were the collection of publisher Robert Clarke and the private Shakespearian library of Cincinnati businessman Enoch Carson, presenting them as the founding book collections for the campus library. Of course, the initial hundreds of volumes in the Carson library have been augmented over the decades with additional rare sets of Shakespeare's plays. For the most part, these books are eighteenth- and nineteenth-century sets of Shakespeare or books on particular aspects of Shakespeare's plays and characters, and most are illustrated. In the twentieth century, fine press editions were acquired as well. And while UC does not own a First Folio, its holdings include some of the most noteworthy editions printed in the last three hundred years.

Enoch Carson was enthralled with William Shakespeare. While this nineteenth-century Cincinnati entrepreneur and civil servant made his fortune in the lamp and gas business, he considered his real wealth to be the hundreds of Shakespeare volumes he accumulated. For the most part, Carson was a self-educated man, attributing his intellectual development to

In this 1920s view of the University of Cincinnati, the domed Van Wormer Library was the first library building on campus, constructed in 1899 and served as the university's main library until 1930.

his years spent reading the plays. So, he devoted his life to building a library of as many editions of the Bard as he could afford. During the 1800s in Europe and America, book lovers scavenged publishers' catalogues, auctions and bookshops to amass their private libraries built on their specific interests. They corresponded at length, trading prints and imprints and finagling to acquire their most desired items. For Carson, the quests were for Masonic books and for Shakespeare. His collection of books on Masonry numbered in the tens of thousands, and while his library of William Shakespeare editions was not quite so large, it was no less impressive for its content.

But he wasn't just a collector—he was a student of the Bard as well and a lover of theatrical performance. In building his library of Shakespeare editions in the many collected works available to him in the nineteenth century, Enoch Carson wanted more than just books. He wanted prints and engravings and sketches as well—anything related to the plays, to Shakespeare's Elizabethan era and to the influences that Shakespeare expressed through his work. This desire on his part was reflective of that transatlantic interest, that drive to acquire the extras that particularly defined one's private library and made it unique. In other words, Enoch Carson was grangerizing his library.

The term refers to extra-illustration and is said to have originated in 1769, when English clergyman James Granger published his catalogue *Biographical History of England from Egbert the Great to the Revolution.* Interestingly, though, Granger's tome did not include any illustrations. What resulted from the publication was that readers of his book began collecting images of the people he listed in it. In the 1800s, this practice became known as *grangerizing*. In essence, people were striving to make a particular book or set of books—Shakespeare, histories, botanical treatises, biographical dictionaries, travel and the like—into their own. In a way, collectors were creating new books, and in that sense what they created were unique collections, something that was special to them and different from everyone else's set of Shakespeare, for example.

The next step after collecting these extra images was to re-create them as full books by disbinding the original volumes and re-binding them to include the additional pages. In many cases, the new versions were sumptuous items with leather bindings and gilded pages. And these were not scrapbooks. Rather, the images were integral to the texts and often used inlaying in paper frames.

As a tribute to the man whose library he purchased, William Procter decided to take all the loose ephemera that Carson accumulated, along with a particular multivolume edition of Shakespeare's works. Before donating the library to UC, Procter took the 1839 Charles Knight edition of Shakespeare's works printed in London—one of the most popular editions—and created a new set. Using the illustrations collected by Carson, Procter had each of the forty-two volumes disbound in order to add the extra engravings and sketches. These illustrations are of a variety of ages and origins, but when bound with the plays they represent, they provide a visual study of the works that were typical of how nineteenth-century productions of Shakespeare have informed how we think about Shakespeare today—costuming, stage sets and scenery. Some are steel or copper engravings; others are pen and ink drawings or aquatints. Many of the volumes include engravings of the notable actors who played the various roles in the eighteenth and nineteenth centuries, and of the latter, many actually performed in Cincinnati, including William Macready, Edwin Forrest, Charles Kean, Charlotte Cushing, Eliza Logan and others.

Enoch Carson's book collecting went well beyond an English playwright, however. In fact, Carson was best known as one of the most important Masons in the country and certainly the most important one in Ohio. There are many photographs of him wearing his regalia as a thirty-third-degree Mason during his work with Scottish Rite Freemasonry, as well as a very interesting photo of him dressed as a knight during the Crusades, complete with chainmail. Carson either founded or was a member of four

Enoch T. Carson, a nineteenth-century Cincinnati businessman and prominent Mason, had a great love of Shakespeare, amassing a huge library of editions and engravings. After his death, Carson's thousands of Masonic volumes were sold to a lodge in New England, but the Shakespeare volumes were purchased by William A. Procter and donated to the University of Cincinnati.

different lodges. In 1884, a portrait of him was commissioned by a Carson Testimonial Committee of the local Masons with a payment of $1,000 to the artist, C.T. Webber. The massive painting measured six and a half by eight and a half feet and was placed in the Scottish Rite Temple on Fifth Street downtown. In the painting, Carson is positioned at his desk, and if you look closely behind him, you can see Hamlet holding the skull of Yorick, paying homage to Carson's favorite play.[10] Shakespeare competed with Masonry to be Enoch Carson's great love, and while his Shakespeare library numbered in the hundreds, it is said that his Masonic library consisted of fifty thousand volumes. At his death in 1899, Carson's Masonic books were supposedly sold to lodges in New England, and his Shakespeare books stayed in Cincinnati through the largesse of William A. Procter. In 1902, just a few years after his death, the local bookselling firm U.P. James put his miscellaneous books, more than one thousand volumes, up for auction. His was an odd library, as listed in the little buff catalogue issued by proprietor Davis L. James in June 1902. Carson's other books ranged from witchcraft, Shakers and humor (those three subjects not combined, you understand) to biography, geography and literature. The listing for his copy of the *Book of the Thousand Nights and One Night* came with this interesting caveat: "Owing to legal causes, the majority of the illustrations were not bound in, but accompanied the work in detached form."[11]

Another great collector was Charles Jacob Livingood, who made his fortune working for the Emery family in Cincinnati, managing their vast real estate holdings. (It was actually Livingood who executed Mary Emery's dream of a model community and created the village of Mariemont in suburban Cincinnati.) As his grandson Virginius Hall remembered him:

> *He always had an enviable motorcar with a chauffeur to drive him.…He never appeared in anything but a three-piece suit with watch chain and stickpin. In winter he wore a bowler hat and a chesterfield overcoat with a velvet collar; in summer he wore a straw boater. His gold pocket watch chimed hours, quarters, and minutes on demand. He seemed to know nearly everybody and everybody called him "Mr. Livingood."*[12]

Livingood married Lily Foster, a descendant of Cincinnati's prominent Lytle family, and they raised their children and grandchildren with a sense of the importance of books. This love of literature inspired Livingood to build several notable collections, filling his Baker Street home. Hall recalled the house:

> *Baker Place wasn't short of books. Every room, upstairs and down, had bookcases. There were two kinds of books, first, the handsomely bound sets of Dickens and Thackeray, Victor Hugo and Macaulay, Fenimore Cooper and Scott, which may or may not have been read, though many assuredly were. Then there were the books—most of them annotated throughout in grandfather's minute red or green printing—that reflected his particular, consuming interests: Petrarch, Dr. Johnson, "prehistorics," as he called the study of prehistoric man, Mistral, southern France, painting, town planning, the Old Northwest and the part played in its history by Lily's family, the Lytles.*

Hall's accounts of his grandfather show Livingood to be a temperamental man of a conservative bent but a devoted bibliophile. And a lucky one, at that: in 1912, he was in England and had a ticket for an ocean liner headed to America. However, he was visiting a bookstore and became so taken with the wonderful books that he missed his voyage. The *Titanic* sailed on without him. Many of Livingood's book collections became part of local libraries. Most of his Petrarch collection was bequeathed to Harvard University, but an outstanding gathering of over one hundred books about the Italian Renaissance humanist ranging from the 1400s to the 1900s went to the University of Cincinnati, as did a collection on James Boswell and Samuel Johnson, the eighteenth-century authors and literary men, donated by his great-granddaughter.

3

PIONEERS OF THE COMICS SECTION AND WRITING IT DOWN

The children are drawn either as freckle-faced street urchins or as the clean-smocked offspring of the hoity-toity. The animals—a parrot, but typically dogs—look on quizzically or crack wise. And the occasion being Valentine's Day, the messages are about the lovelorn and the hopeful. These are the early twentieth-century postcards drawn by R.F. Outcault, a pioneer of the modern newspaper comic strip who gave America such literary figures as Buster Brown and the Yellow Kid. And advertising being what it was, Buster and the Kid gave us books, shoes, coin banks, calendars, clocks, pencils, puzzles and all manner of geegaws, selling the country on the all-American pastime of buying stuff. The postcards deviated from the overall merchandising a bit, although Outcault's newspaper employers and their agents certainly generated a lot of them. The holiday cards were something a little different, a reflection of the artist's own attitudes to his comics. They were his "O! Will I be your Valentine" creations, all with a touch of rejected affection. His other comics contrasted the clean clothes and misbehavior of Buster Brown and his dog Tige with the rough neighborhood of Mickey Dugan in Hogan's Alley, playing on the contrast between Irish American tenement life and that of the indulged and privileged.

Richard Felton Outcault was born in 1863 in Lancaster, Ohio, and came to Cincinnati in 1878 to attend the McMicken School of Design, which through a series of changes and mergers is now the Cincinnati Art Academy.

After graduating in 1881, he got a job painting pretty rural scenes in the huge office safes manufactured by the Hall Safe and Lock Company, and with his local reputation growing, he extended his talent a bit and submitted some cartoons to Joseph Pulitzer and the *New York World.* He also painted scenery and posters for the 1888 centennial industrial exposition in Cincinnati, one of the many local product fairs held in the nineteenth century that were begun as an outlet for the Ohio Mechanics Institute. He specifically worked on Thomas Edison's electric light displays, parlaying that into a career on the East Coast with trade magazines like the *Electrical World*. Edison later sent Outcault to Paris for the World's Fair, and he took advantage of the situation to study art there. When he returned, Outcault settled in New York City. By 1894, he was drawing cartoons on a regular basis for newspapers and magazines like *Judge* and *Life*, the *New York World* and the *New York Journal.* It was at this time that he created his first famous character of his *Hogan's Alley* cartoon, the Yellow Kid. By 1902, R.F. had introduced his Buster Brown character with the faithful terrier Tige. And his personal style of using panels and dialogue balloons became a standard in cartooning.

His cartoons, like his Valentine postcards, were unlike the typical sweet and lovey-dovey cards of today. There was an edge to his art, a bit of an insult here and there and more rejection than true love. In a way, Outcault's cartoons were an outgrowth of the so-called Vinegar Valentines of Victorian America. Vinegar Valentines were sarcastic and insulting, greetings designed to reject the offers of true love. Competing with true romantic Valentines, these little missives of misanthropy usually were sent anonymously to those persons one disliked, be they flirtatious bachelors or suffragists. Outcault's cards resembled them in a natural progression, one supposes, from invective to just strange little takes on the whole idea of Valentine's Day.

With his innovative cartoon style, refining the use of multiple panels and thought balloons, Outcault had a long and productive cartooning career. After retiring from the hubbub of daily newspaper work, he spent the last decade of his life quietly painting and died in 1928.

Another Cincinnati cartoonist is honored with one of the city's great building murals, a panel from *Little Nemo in Slumberland* at 917 Main Street. Little Nemo was the creation of Winsor McCay, who came to Cincinnati from Chicago in 1891. McCay lived in Cincinnati for nine years, working for the many dime or street museums in the city like Heck & Avery's Family Theater and its offshoots, Avery's New Dime Museum, Will S. Heck's Wonder World & Theater, as well as the Kohl and Middleton Museum. McCay painted backdrops, posters and advertisements for the museums,

As part of ArtWorks Cincinnati's building murals throughout the city, pioneering cartoon strip artist Winsor McCay was honored in 2016 with his "Little Nemo in Slumberland" at 917 Main Street. Under teaching assistants Mary Claus and Kena Dillon and project manager Tim Parsley, the mural employed ten youth apprentices and is part of the Cincinnati Masters Mural Series.

developing such a popular following that crowds of people would gather on the street to watch him paint the ads. He also experimented with architectural renderings of a sort, drawing a revised layout of the University of Cincinnati campus, complete with gargoyles, griffins and a massive wall surrounding the buildings.

But it was when he was employed at Heck's Wonder World that he had an opportunity to see Thomas Edison's Vitascope in operation, an event that inspired him to experiment later with animated films, much of the style of which was drawn from his cartoon work. As he was doing freelance work for the *Cincinnati Commercial Tribune* and the *Cincinnati Enquirer*, McCay tried a cartoon, *A Tale of the Jungle Imps by Felix Fiddle.* With this new direction in his art, McCay moved to New York in the mid-1890s, doing illustrations and editorial cartoons for the *New York Herald.* Interestingly, he found himself working alongside R.F. Outcault, which turned somewhat bitter and led to Outcault leaving the paper and moving back to his previous employer, the *New York Journal.* By 1904, McCay was drawing regular comic strips like *Little Sammy Sneeze* and one of his greatest successes, *Dream of the Rarebit Fiend*, a bizarre comic in which characters had terrifying dreams resulting from a dinner of Welsh rarebit. In 1905, he created *Little Nemo in Slumberland*, the cartoon that would come to be seen as his masterpiece. Again, McCay used the theme of fantastic dreams for Nemo, but the content of the cartoon was only part of his success with it. He used different visual perspectives and different sized panels to tell the story, an innovation that readers accepted with great favor. It was animation that really captured McCay's interests, however. Basing his films on the flip books that his children read, McCay produced ten animated films between 1911 and 1921. More than four thousand drawings were made for his first film, which featured Little Nemo. He combined his films with a vaudeville act he developed, interacting with another celluloid character he developed, Gertie the Dinosaur. McCay died in 1934 and is buried in Brooklyn.

The world of poetry in Cincinnati has the range of other cities of its age: the newspaper and postcard doggerel alternately raises a quick smile or angry frown, the civic "boosterism" poems that are more about being "firstest or "bestest," the literary lines of committed working poets or the light verse thrown together for various clubs or causes. Of this latter, one of the best was the publication issued by the Sinners Club of Cincinnati in 1922.[13] Titled *Blue Law Ballads: A Purge for Puritans*, the book was copyrighted by a William C. Smith, who also put together an earlier volume, now lost, called *Jazz Bible Lyrics*. In *Blue Law Ballads*, the Sinners took on blue-nose citizens, Prohibition, evangelists and anyone else who would deny them their hedonistic pleasures. Some of the more interesting poems had titles like "My Lady Nicotine," "In Praise of Profanity," "The Amorous Russian" and "Inventors of Hell." In "Sons of the Cup," the poet says:

Tipsy old topers,
Jolly old dopers,
Blessed and bibulous sons of the cup,
Sit up and listen,
Aid me to christen,
The loveliest lyric since Hec was a pup.

Cock-tails and high-balls
Were Beauty's first rivals
Ever since Noah came out of his ship
Nothing's so handy
As soda and brandy
To drive us along at a merry old clip.

When Life's confusing,
And we are losing
Out in the struggle for honors and rep,
Burgundy, Sherry
Help us grow merry,
Fill us with ginger and load us with pep.

Oft when Ambition
Fails of its mission
And we're so weary, we don't care a rap,
Wine, Beer, and Whiskey
Make us feel frisky
Saturate all of our being with Snap.

The poems are quite well-written, obviously by sinners of some intelligence. Their identities are unknown, unless there are descendants somewhere about Cincinnati who can reveal the poets behind the signatures they used in distributing books to their friends: "the Arch Fiend," "the Lariat," "the Artist" and "Rabelais." It's interesting to read one poem of theirs, "Sahara," that mocks Prohibition but refers back several decades to a well-known Cincinnati poet and his most famous verse, "Antony and Cleopatra," using his line, "I am dying, Egypt, dying!" Their inspiration was a soldier-poet of a devastating American conflict.[14]

On September 20, 1863, in the midst of the Civil War, General William Haines Lytle of Cincinnati was shot and killed by a Confederate sniper's bullet in the Battle of Chickamauga. A few days later, his body was carried back to his hometown, and his funeral was held at Christ Church Cathedral in downtown Cincinnati. Thousands of mourners followed his casket in the cortege to Spring Grove Cemetery, miles away from the church. The slow procession took up most of the day, and the general's body did not arrive at Spring Grove until dusk. Sometime later, his grave marker—a broken column symbolizing a life cut short—would dominate the landscape of the garden cemetery.

William Lytle was more than another military officer killed in battle. He was a literary man, a soldier-poet whose verse in antebellum America was popular in both the North and the South and whose lines reflected his experiences on the battlefield. His words showed a view of the bloody vista typical of the early nineteenth century in which he was educated, and they embodied his view of duty as well as a life of purpose. In Lytle's eyes, war revealed a terrible beauty of death and destruction. He was a part of the Romantic tradition in his poetry, incorporating his classical studies as a boy with his notions of heroism and direction in life. An excerpt from a poem he wrote in 1840 as a fourteen-year-old, "The Soldier's Death," illustrates his early grasp of duty:

Early in the morning we found him lying cold and stiff on
the scene of his former exploits

The night had come and the stars were bright,
And the moon shone o'er the battlefield,
When the unjust cause of a tyrant's might
Was crushed by the weight of freedom's shield…

Upon the waste so stained with blood,
Beside a great and rushing stream,
A worn and weary soldier stood,
Like a phantom raised in a feverish dream…

When mortals by the wayside passed,
The soldier's last deep breath had flown,
With naught to cheer save the midnight blast,
On the battlefield had he died—alone.

William Lytle was born in 1826 into a prominent Cincinnati family and educated at Cincinnati College, founded in 1819 and to which the University of Cincinnati traces its heritage. He later studied for the law and established a practice in the city. But during his early legal career, Lytle maintained a sense of wonder about the world and a desire to achieve satisfaction on the battlefield because he was enamored of the concept of "heroic death." His life, he felt, should emulate that of Greek heroes and Shakespearean warriors. When the Mexican-American War broke out in 1846, Lytle enlisted in the Second Ohio Volunteer Infantry and served as a captain. During the conflict, he continued his writing, constructing poetry in the notion of a heroic vein. The verses from his image of one battle during that war, "The Siege of Chapultepec," show this bent in his approach to poetry:

Wide o'er the valley the pennons are fluttering,
War's sullen story the deep guns are muttering,
Forward! blue-jackets in good steady order,
Strike for the fame of your good northern border;
Forever shall history tell of the bloody check
Waiting the foe at the siege of Chapultepec…

…Death revels high in the midst of the bloody sport…

And on one general, T.L. Hamer:

The brave who sleep in glory's shroud,
How proud a fate is theirs!

After he returned to Cincinnati from Mexico, Lytle continued to build his law practice and successfully ran for election to the Ohio state legislature. But poetry became his passion, and as he published more of it in anthologies and newspapers, he became quite popular on both sides of the Mason-Dixon line. This popularity would realize a significance in his eventual death.

When the Civil War broke out in 1861, William Lytle was commissioned as a colonel in the Tenth Ohio Volunteer Regiment, a regiment composed primarily of working-class Irish in Cincinnati. His troops mustered in nearby Camp Dennison, and soon they were dispatched to the Virginia battlefields. The regiment became known, in a tip to an Irish brogue, as the "Bloody Tinth" for its actions. For Lytle, whose verse had been widely recited before the war, his embracing of classical heroism and duty were rendered as lamentations about the battlefield. This mindset of his was evident even in his letters home to his treasured sisters before he led his men into battle at Carnifex Ferry in Virginia in 1861:

> *My beloved Sisters,*
>
> *It is very late at night but I could not sleep without writing to you. An engagement is expected very soon—probably tomorrow. I am not at liberty to give particulars—except that I heard tonight unofficially that my regiment would have the advance....Good bye my darling sisters. I hope a merciful God may re-unite us in this world, but if otherwise ordered let us hope to meet in a better one.*

During that battle, albeit a minor skirmish, Lytle's men suffered many casualties. The colonel took a bullet in his calf that resulted in a serious wound and sent him back home to Cincinnati for an extended recovery. When he returned to service, he resumed his customary approach to a battlefield fate, expressed again in a letter to his sisters that stated his love and his sense of duty. Lytle's letters were not dissimilar from that of thousands of other soldiers who were writing home to their loved ones, but he seemed to thrive in the style and the literary tradition he acutely knew he embodied in his writings. As he returned to fighting in Kentucky and Virginia, he penned this letter to one of his sisters:

> *Would be to God dear Sister this unhappy war were honorably terminated.... And yet I feel it my duty as long as I can to share with my generation its heavy burden and to stand along side of my brave comrades in arms to the last gasp....In no nobler or holier a cause can a man's life be offered up.... Farewell dear Bessie.*

He wrote this poem, "In Camp," in 1862:

> *I gazed forth from my wintry tent*
> *Upon the star-gemmed firmament...*

I gazed, till to the sun the drums
Rolled at the dawn, "He comes, he comes."

Though he held to the tropes of death, destruction and devastation on the battlefields that spread out before him, Lytle's writing most often turned to himself in almost a narcissistic manner of how he answered the call or entered the fray and was he up to snuff as a Greek hero, was he executing his duty as a Roman centurion, was he mindful enough of his responsibility to his soldiers and to his family as an American, would he fall on the stage of bloody ground as well and as dignified in death as a Shakespeare tragedian? The field of battle became his dramatic stage.

Lytle was wounded once more in the war. It was the second time, and though it is tempting to read his verse as poetic posturing of a sort, in the view of his friends, family and countrymen who read his poems with love and admiration, he was indeed courageous and never hesitant in putting himself in harm's way as he led his troops across the fought-for fields and mountain passes. His promotion to brigadier general earned him more responsibility along with a heavy-hearted acceptance and, perhaps, appreciation of his own duty.

His time was coming. In September 1863, at Chickamauga Creek in Georgia, he led his troops in a counterattack against the Confederate line. Just days before, even though he had some time ago been reassigned to other regiments, the Tenth Ohio Volunteer Regiment, his old troop of Irish fighters, presented him with a bejeweled Maltese cross for his leadership. In the counterattack around midday, a sniper's bullet found him. Knowing who he was, the Rebel troops held his body and respectfully placed a guard around him for the night, quietly reciting his poetry. In a brief truce the next day, Lytle's corpse was carried forward to his Union troops, and he was sent home for burial.

Lytle was mourned by both sides of the conflict, his battle poetry and verse of man against man—and man against fate—loved by both sides because in many ways the poems answered a need to be noble in life. There was a shared cultural background in this respect. His poetry was a reflection of popular form and subject. The blood and gore of the Civil War may have signaled the end of a reliance on—and an education in—the Romantic form.

As those Confederate soldiers guarded Lytle's body the night of his death, the verse that was read was one of his most well-known, a poem he wrote in 1858 titled "Antony and Cleopatra":

I am dying, Egypt, dying!
Hark! the insulting foeman's cry;
They are coming; quick, my falchion!
Let me front them ere I die.
Ah, no more amid the battle
Shall my heart exulting swell;
Isis and Osiris guard thee,—
Cleopatra, Rome, farewell!

Fast-forward to the Sinners Club and the twentieth century and the emergence of the journalist-poet George Elliston. As background to her name, Elliston's parents were expecting a boy, had settled on a name and were not about to change it when Mother Elliston gave birth to a girl. In adulthood, George became quite an admired journalist, a reporter who was tough as nails and could spit the same. As he came to know her in the 1930s and '40s, Ellis Rawnsley, editor and reporter the *Cincinnati Times-Star*, often recalled his colleague saying that as police approached the front of a building where a murder had taken place, Elliston was already climbing in a back window to get a first look at the victim and the crime scene. And while she seemingly lived the miser's life, cadging meals from friends and eating the basest of dinners when she couldn't, living in cold-water flats and dressing in old clothes, the truth was that Elliston maintained a cabin where she could get away with her friends to stage little musical performances and read poetry. She was a remarkably attractive woman, though few people saw her features beneath the cloche hat she frequently wore, and she was often wrapped in an old overcoat. Elliston's passion in life was poetry, and she published several volumes of her own verse. In one volume, *Changing Moods*, published in 1922 by the Sign of the Pen and Pad Press in Cincinnati, she has a beautiful poem called "Quiet Streets":

Some live in quiet streets
And naught of all the noise and sound
Touches their consciousness.
They live serene, aloof, profound
Unto themselves, but out
Of traffic's dim and mad dismay,
Their only contact with
This world as with a foreign fray
Seen in a dream, unreal, untrue.[15]

George (yes, George) Elliston was the ever-intrepid reporter for the *Times-Star* who thrived on crime journalism. Her true love was poetry, however, and she published several volumes. Elliston lived like a miser, and when she died, she bequeathed a fortune to the University of Cincinnati to found a modern poetry collection.

She could have been writing of herself. When George Elliston died in 1946, she bequeathed $250,000 to the University of Cincinnati to "promote the cause of poetry." With its poets-in-residence program attracting prestigious poets from America and Great Britain and the building of a library of modern poetry, Elliston's dream was realized.

In recent years, the City of Cincinnati established a poet laureate program, first with the poet Pauletta Hansel in 2016 and Latino poet Manuel Iris in 2018. The purpose of the program is to name a poet whose poetry speaks of the multiculturalism and spirit of the city, promote the love of reading poetry and encourage the writing of poetry, as well as to use the two-year appointment to write poetry for special Cincinnati events. Iris's appointment was significant because of the growing Latino population in Cincinnati, helping embrace a new element of its population, and Hansel's tenure reflected a long-standing Appalachian population, evidenced today by her own poetry as well as that of others like Richard Hague and Ben Kline, both of whom have Appalachian roots but approach their own poetry from vastly different directions. Poetry is the richest expression of literary endeavors in

Cincinnati, with several open mic nights and spoken word events, Mercantile Library readings and study groups led by poet Norman Finkelstein and the poetry slam programs of Kimberly "DuWaup" Bolden.

Beyond poetry and cartooning, the heritage of journalism and fiction is a rich part of Cincinnati literature. Journalism in Cincinnati, for example, during the 1800s was similar to that of newspapers, magazines and books that were published around the country. Accounts by German travelers often spoke of the practical ins and outs of settling in Cincinnati, of the weather, business opportunities and education that awaited them. And accounts by visitors who stopped in Cincinnati during their American tours often spoke of the ethnic groups they found here. One example is that of author Charles Dickens. Dickens's visit to Cincinnati in 1842 was part of the itinerary on his first journey to America, with initial stops in Boston, New York, Washington and Pittsburgh.

Accompanied by his wife, Catherine, Dickens thoroughly enjoyed Boston, was not so enthralled by the nation's capital with all the heated politics and had quite a negative impression of Pittsburgh. Cincinnati in springtime, however, he found to be "a beautiful city, cheerful, thriving, and animated." Dickens documented his trip to the United States in *American Notes for General Circulation*, published in October 1842 after his return to England.[16] In Cincinnati, he was very complimentary about the orderly streets and houses, so it is apparent that he wasn't walking about during one of the regular hog drives to the slaughterhouses. He enjoyed the view from Mount Auburn, complimented the city's system of free schools and sat in on a nuisance trial in the courts. In *American Notes*, he stated: "The society with which I mingled was intelligent, courteous, and agreeable."

One occasion that really caught his fancy was an Irish temperance parade through downtown, organized by local followers of the Irish temperance leader Father Theobald Mathew, who at the time was in his abstinence glory across the ocean in Cork. Dickens noted,

> *I was particularly pleased to see the Irishmen, who formed a distinct society among themselves, and mustered very strong with their green scarfs carrying their national harp and their Portrait of Father Mathew high above the people's heads. They looked as jolly and good-humoured as ever; and, working (here) the hardest for their living, and doing any kind of sturdy labor that came in their way, were the most independent fellows there, I thought.*

After Cincinnati, Dickens continued his travels west, to Louisville and St. Louis. But the more he traveled, the more disaffected he became with America. The journey was wearing on him, and he was tiring of the people and the frontier. On his return to Cincinnati to head east and then to sail for London, the rough coach ride on the corduroy road from Cincinnati to Lake Erie nearly did him in, along with sleeping in insect-infested cabins. When it was published, *American Notes* came under criticism from some American readers who felt Dickens maligned their fair country. And even though the book waxed enthusiastically about Cincinnati, in a private letter to a friend, Dickens confessed that at a party, a judge introduced him to "at least one hundred and fifty first-rate bores" and that he thought his face "has acquired a fixed expression of sadness from the constant and unmitigated boring I endure." Perhaps he should have joined the Irishmen who were not in the temperance march.

One of the many playwrights who lived for a time in nineteenth-century Cincinnati was the Irish author Dionysius Lardner Boucicault. While he was a resident in 1855, he wrote *Grimaldi: Or, Scenes in the Life of an Actress*, starring his second wife, Agnes Robertson. His first wife died very mysteriously just before he moved to America.

Cincinnati not only drew comments about its Irish citizens but also attracted Irish writers and actors on a regular basis. In the mid-1850s, Irish playwright Dionysius Lardner Boucicault came to Cincinnati to write and produce plays for the National Theater. His arrival was not without speculation and gossip, however. Boucicault came to the United States in his elopement with Agnes Robertson, an actress he had come to know shortly after the very mysterious death of his first wife when they were in Switzerland together. However the tides of local gossip ebbed and flowed around him, he found enthusiastic audiences in Cincinnati. Boucicault produced several plays here, sometimes acting in some of them himself, but nearly all of them starring Agnes. One of his hits was *Grimaldi: Or, Scenes in the Life of an Actress* (featuring Agnes) that he debuted at the National Theater in September 1855.

Cincinnati was not shy of theaters in those days. There were quite a few of them, offering up English and Irish plays, the classics and light comedies. Theatergoers had their pick on most nights. And there was always plenty of scandal that made life interesting. The People's Theater, for example, quickened the impression staid Cincinnatians had of Irish life in the city. One night in 1846, a backstage love match descended into violence. It seems there was a "danseuse" by the name of Mrs. Cook (neither her nor her husband's first names would ever be revealed) who attracted the attention of an Irish comedian, John Reeve. Reeve embraced her charms, and when Mr. Cook discovered the affair, he enlisted the assistance of the theater's treasurer, accosted Reeve and killed him with a knife to the heart. That evening's performance was canceled. Mr. Cook hightailed it out of town, and the management of the rival National Theater offered a reward for his capture. But was the cuckolded husband ever apprehended? The follow-up reports are vague.

Another Irishman made his literary mark in Cincinnati. During the Cincinnati winter of 1874, over 140 years ago, a half-blind, half-Irish little figure of a man wrote this for the *Cincinnati Enquirer*:

> *It is in all times a rugged road to the Place of Nameless Graves—a road running over rolling ground, where vehicles rock from side to side like ships in a gale and groan in all their timbers. "Rattle his bones over the stones, He's only a pauper whom nobody owns." Hundreds of paupers' bones are rattled over that road every year: the Undertaker always sending out three or four at a time in a covered wagon, with frightfully stiff springs. And as the dismal vehicle rolls along the coffins rattle and bump one against the other fearfully from side to side, and bump horribly against the thinly-lined walls of those long and ghastly boxes.*

Lafcadio Hearn's article "Golgotha, A Pilgrimage to Potter's Field," was written for the November 29 issue that year. Hearn, who would chronicle the lowlifes, ghosts and murderers of Cincinnati for several years before moving on to New Orleans, eventually settled in Japan, where even today he is revered as a major literary figure. But he made his journalistic mark in Cincinnati because he went where other journalists would not, exploring the alleys and tenements and riverside settlements that housed the city's worst and most colorful citizens. He delved into the lives of petty criminals and opium addicts, of mysterious mediums and fast-talking flim-flam men, as well as the cops and saloonkeepers who dealt with the underbelly of

Authors Grove in Eden Park began in 1882 as a public school effort to plant trees and honor America's authors with plaques and annual ceremonies. Today, the trees still beautify the park, but the only "remains" of the authors is a partial brick wall and a granite book.

Cincinnati society. And he did it by just letting them tell their stories, by insinuating himself in his own reporting, by writing in the authentic dialect of the storytellers he courted and by thrilling his readers nearly every day with a world in which they would seldom—or never—visit.

Hearn had this to say about himself in Cincinnati:

> *Now in those days there was a young man connected with the* Daily Enquirer *whose tastes were whimsically grotesque and arabesque. He was by nature a fervent admirer of extremes. He believed only in the Revoltingly Horrible or the Excruciatingly Beautiful. He worshipped the French school of sensation, and reveled in thrusting a reeking mixture of bones, blood and hair under peoples' noses at breakfast time.*

So how did this diminutive Irishman happen to appear in Cincinnati? Christened Patrick Lafcadio Hearn, he was born in 1850 in the Greek islands, specifically Lefkada, to Charles Bush Hearn of County Offaly, Ireland, and a Greek woman, Rosa Kassimati. Hearn's father was a surgeon in the British army when Great Britain controlled those islands. Lafcadio's parents were married in the Greek Orthodox Church, and he was baptized into that faith as well.

The family's circumstances did not turn out well on that Greek island, and when his father was transferred to the British West Indies, his family was left behind. Hearn's mother managed to get to Ireland but abandoned her son to the care of a paternal great-aunt, Sarah Brenane. After 1857, Hearn never saw his parents again. In Ireland, he was afforded a classical education that was later carried on in France, where he became fluent in the language, and his Irish relations later enrolled him in school in England. It was in England that he lost the vision in his left eye at the age of sixteen due to a schoolyard accident, and as he suffered from severe myopia anyway, for the rest of his life Hearn turned his head so as to avoid people seeing his injured eye, instead letting them focus on his bulging right eye.

By 1867, the Brenane fortune that supported him had dissipated, and he found himself in London's East End, where he wandered the streets and visited libraries and museums. However, his great-aunt's family managed to recover some of its money, so a one-way ticket to New York was presented to the young Hearn and he was instructed to make his way to Cincinnati, where a family benefactor might assist him in finding work. As he later said in a biographical piece, "I was dropped moneyless on the pavement of an American city to begin life."

At first, Hearn lived in the alleys and stables in Cincinnati, taking on whatever work he could find. Eventually, he found employment with a local printer, Henry Watkin, who kindly encouraged him to keep studying, so Hearn made wide use of Watkin's personal library as well as Cincinnati's public library. By 1872, he had landed a job as a reporter for the *Enquirer*, where he remained until 1875.

At the time Hearn arrived in Cincinnati, there were about twenty thousand Irish immigrants living in the city. In the decades since the city's founding in the late 1700s, the social and economic status of the city's Irish population varied widely, from the wealth and influence of families like the Gambles, the Sintons and the Pogues, who owned factories and stores, to the working-class families in the neighborhoods of Fulton and Mount Adams and the impoverished families along the slums of the Ohio River basin. And that became the perfect milieu for someone like Hearn, who had no particular loyalty to his ethnic brothers and sisters, though he did revel in the secrets and dark tales of anyone who was even below this hoi polloi, not to mention the hoity-toity. Known as a sensationalistic journalist, Hearn relished the idea of giving upper-class readers of the daily newspaper a taste of the sordid lives they otherwise shunned every day. He lived for the lurid.

Lafcadio Hearn, the Irish-Greek author who became a major literary figure in Japan, began his career as a journalist in Cincinnati in 1872 where he arrived in poverty, departed in scandal and in between regaled newspaper readers with lively tales of ghosts, murderers and flim-flam men.

So Lafcadio Hearn's writing career blossomed in the Queen City, and in 1874, he met Henry Farny, who later gained fame for his Western paintings. The two published a tabloid called *Ye Giglampz*, a weekly that Hearn wrote and Farny illustrated. The publication's articles chronicled the cultural happenings in Cincinnati along with satirical commentary, but it lasted all of nine issues before folding. *Ye Giglampz* was published at a time when such tabloids were becoming mainstream in American cities. Another local example was *Sam the Scaramouch*, which came along just a decade later in 1884—it, too, was short-lived. Satire sometimes makes enemies of readers and those who control credit and purse strings.

In that same year, 1874, Hearn married Mattie Foley, who was African American, and because of what the *Enquirer* management termed his "illegal marriage," as well as the paper having to fend off local clerical criticism of Hearn's writings, the newspaper fired him. Hearn immediately went to the rival *Cincinnati Commercial*, where he worked another three years. The result of his reporting is that Hearn can be credited for being one of the first American journalists to capture the essence of African American lives and to render their speech and song lyrics in a realistic way.

So by 1877, after writing more than four hundred stories and essays for Cincinnati papers, Hearn grew weary of the city, and with the blessing of the *Commercial*'s editor, he moved to New Orleans. He sent dispatches to the Cincinnati paper while at the same time penning articles for *Harper's Weekly* and the *New Orleans Times Democrat.* He stayed in New Orleans for a decade as his writing career flowered, and he published several books on proverbs, Creole life and folklore, indulging his penchant for ghost stories and the macabre. In this regard, the city of New Orleans with its romantic strangeness was perfect for him.

Following his life in New Orleans, Hearn spent a couple of years in the West Indies as a correspondent before moving to Japan in 1890; he lived there for the remainder of his life. He died in 1904 at the age of fifty-four. In Japan, Hearn became a teacher, married a Japanese woman (he and Foley were long divorced) and had four children. His greatest literary achievement was rendering the unknown society of Japan to Western readers in a lucid and vibrant manner in several books on Japanese culture, especially folklore and fairy tales. He took the name Koizumi Yakumo, and his reputation as a storyteller in their lives endeared him to the Japanese. Since his death, there have been multiple anthologies of his works in Japan, and there are monuments and a museum dedicated to him as well. Postage stamps are adorned with his image, and there are many Lafcadio Hearn literary societies.

The two major repositories of Hearn material in the United States are at Tulane University and the Public Library of Cincinnati and Hamilton County.

But back to this Irishman in Cincinnati: other writers in the 1800s chronicled the local Irish life, such as Boucicault and, of course, Dickens. It was Hearn who most fully explored Irish life here, in large measure because he was a resident rather than visiting literati like Dickens and Boucicault. Though he relished the idea of shocking his readers, the notion that his human subjects represented the most interesting aspects of Cincinnati society was very real to him, be they pickpockets, whores, grifters, body snatchers, singers and dancers, ghosts and ghouls or even murderers. Hearn's masterpiece of Cincinnati macabre was his reporting on the Tanyard killing, a murder that journalist and Hearn scholar Jon Hughes covered with his monograph, *The Tanyard Murder: On the Case with Lafcadio Hearn.*[17] The murder in question took place in November 1874 in a neighborhood called "The Shambles," that stretch of slaughterhouses along the Miami-Erie Canal near Central Avenue and Findlay Street.

As Hearn described it,

> *It is a quarter where the senses of sight and hearing and smell are at once assailed with all the foulnesses of the charnel-house and the shambles. It is the center of all those trades which harden and brutalized the men who engage in them.*

After a fire at the Werk candle factory, a body was discovered across the street in the Freiberg Tannery. A German immigrant, Herman Schilling, was murdered by Andreas Egner, his son Frederic Egner and a third man, George Rufer. The elder Egner became enraged because Schilling was dallying with his daughter, Julia Egner, fifteen years old and with a compromised reputation. So Schilling was strangled, run through with a pitchfork and thrown into the boiler of the tannery, in which his skull burst. But his teeth, as Hearn described them, remained "ghastly white." Hearn's reporting made the front page of the *Enquirer*, and he continued the story for two weeks, causing a national sensation because of the grisly woodcuts that accompanied it. It was said that Schilling had been thrown into the fire while he was still alive. The perpetrators were caught, tried and convicted. Hearn reported:

> *Certainly the dogs used not to howl so before last Saturday night. How they could have quieted while the hideous tragedy was being enacted, hearing the dull, skull-crushing blows, the death struggle: the shrieks for aid, the body dragged from the stable to the furnace, leaving its blood-trail behind, the strangely horrible crackling and spluttering and hissing within the furnace, is something very difficult to comprehend.*

With the Tanyard murder, Hearn was in his element, at once thrilling and repelling his morning readers and thereby forming his literary reputation in Cincinnati.

Not many years after *Ye Giglampz* failed and Lafcadio Hearn lit out for New Orleans, another tabloid was born to titillate and shock Cincinnati readers. For thirteen months between February 1885 and February 1886, a tabloid publication in Cincinnati published a wide range of articles, cartoons, editorials and stories that lampooned American life. No topic or person escaped the sharp wit of *Sam the Scaramouch*, and for the short time this weekly newspaper was in existence, its editors took on national tariffs, elections from Cincinnati to Washington, the temperance issue, urban sophisticates and country bumpkins, race and ethnicity and a growing national obsession with sports. Grover Cleveland was president. European colonization of Africa was in full force. The Statue of Liberty arrived in New York, and Ulysses S. Grant died. And, in many ways, *Sam* was like other newspapers around the country in covering these events, carrying local advertisements and notices and publishing occasional doggerel and short fiction, reflecting the "new" journalistic realism.

Sam the Scaramouch was the brainchild of three Cincinnatians: Peter Gibson Thomson, C.V. Van Hamm and Absalom H. Mattox. Thomson was a manufacturer of toys, books and games, as well as a printer. One of his children's books, for example, was a lavishly illustrated and heavily adapted edition of Shakespeare's plays. Mattox was a commercial clerk, while Van Hamm's regular occupation is unknown. Together, the three of them incorporated their little newspaper and published it out of a building on Vine Street in Cincinnati's Over-the-Rhine, the predominantly German neighborhood at the time. Their pieces in *Sam*, either written by themselves or solicited from other like-minded gentlemen, were sharply written, disrespectful, irreverent and funny—everything one could ask of satire. They took their title from a stock character in nineteenth-century Italian theater: "Scaramouch" referred to a boastful, cowardly buffoon, and by the latter part of the century, the term had also come to mean a rascal or scamp. Where the "Sam" part came from, no one knows. Perhaps the editors were just taken with the nice alliteration.

In addition to political issues and international affairs, the editors also directed their barbs at the differences between urban and rural America and at the racial and ethnic groups dwelling in the nation's cities. As one might expect in a city that was heavily German in 1885, that particular ethnic group came under a great deal of lampooning, with cartoons and dialect stories emphasizing every stereotype from shabby, lecherous Germans accosting young girls outside saloons to the beginning of various sausage "seasons." But African Americans, Jews, the Irish, the English and the Italians were all subject to weekly barbs. The intended readership appears to be those citizens who were educated, politically informed, socially aloof, white, male

A hillside view of Cincinnati in the 1870s, when the city was one of the nation's largest centers for printing and publishing and engravings were a prominent part the Queen City's reputation in the graphic arts.

and professional. Dialogue in the articles and in the fiction were in dialect. No one was spared; everyone was set up to be offended.

In 1885, a quirky little tale was published in *Sam the Scaramouch.* The anonymously written story is titled "O'Toole's Ghost" and its plot centers on a young immigrant by the name of Mickey McGonigle who dreams of becoming the best baseball player ever seen. Late one night, he is visited by the ghost of a deceased pitcher by the name of Barney O'Toole, who offers to fulfill this dream on one small condition: never argue with the umpire. McGonigle accepts the offer, and for a brief time, he is indeed the greatest player in the land.

> *"Whist, Mickey!" said the shade. "Me gossoon, yez are the laddie to take me place. Do as I told yes, omadhaun, and yez will become famous."*
>
> *The vision seemed to be smiling…"Musha, yez blackguard, only hould yer tongue whin the umpire decides agin yer, and yer will become a great player. So long as yer no kicker agin an umpire, so long will ye prosper and make home runs. Don't moind the bat, me boy; let her fly, and she will make four-base hits every pop. But moind, yes blackguard, but make a single kick against the umpire, yer gone…do yez hear?"*

But during one game, he forgets that agreed-on condition with the ghost, violates it by coming to bat and disputing balls and strikes with the umpire and sees his prowess quickly and publicly stripped away. He spends the rest of his days consumed with regret and humiliation, pushing an ash cart through the streets of Cincinnati.

On a simple look, "O'Toole's Ghost" is a trifle of a tale, complete with all the elements of modern baseball in terms of ethnicity, carping against the umpire and the avarice of owners. The only thing changed over a century later is the scale of finances. But it points to an element of American literature that is often repeated in male-oriented fiction: the visitation of ghosts who can either create or restore the masculinity and social standing of a character through sporting achievement. The theme reflects a peculiar national concern with the definition and expression of masculinity, that is, the male validation or nonmale rejection that arose in an immigrant culture consumed with a confluence of ethnic identity, individuality, group behavior, self-expression of authority and achievement over a perceived loss of manhood—with the American hope of a chance at redemption in the social order. We like to believe that even with the intervention of the supernatural, our own ethic will triumph in the end—or at least often enough that we keep the faith.

In examining the plot elements of such stories and novels, we discover a sense of loss—or a lost opportunity—that threatens to leave the characters without the means to carry themselves successfully through stages of male camaraderie, sexual mating to create a home of an admiring wife and adoring children and achieving the American dream. That is, unless they welcome an intervention by the spirits of those who have gone before, like Barney O'Toole. In such a society, however, bargains must be struck; it is a quid pro quo Faustian arrangement, financial success with the failure of fulfillment being a living and miserable "hell" on earth.

Beyond all the analytical back-and-forth, "O'Toole's Ghost" is just a funny story, and it precedes by a full three years Ernest Lawrence Thayer's classic doggerel "Casey at the Bat," with the same elements of failed Irish heroics, which was published in the *San Francisco Examiner* in 1888.

Just a few years before *Sam the Scaramouch* began its short life, Dublin author and aesthete Oscar Wilde gave Cincinnatians a further impression of the Irish talent for literary life and a stage. In February 1882, Wilde took that stage at the Grand Opera House to share his opinions on "the decorative arts." The Cincinnati stop was part of his American tour, and local Wilde fans bought the Wilde-inspired clothing and jewelry marketed by the city's department stores. The Irishman reportedly liked Cincinnati and his hosts a great deal, but his second lecture in the city that June met with tedium and tepid reactions.

A generation later, in 1917, Cincinnati was again in the forefront of news, but it wasn't generated from the homefront. The noted journalist and philologist H.L. Mencken published an article in the *New York Evening Mail* concerning the history of the bathtub in the United States. According to the Baltimore writer, known as much for his satire and acerbic wit as he was for his political reporting, Cincinnati was home to this tub. Mencken asserted that America's first bathtub was introduced on December 20, 1842, by Adam Thompson, who lived in Cincinnati, Ohio, of all places. Made of mahogany and lined with lead, the vessel was introduced by Thompson to his guests at a Christmas party where he described how it worked and invited the partygoers to take a dip. Four of them took him up on his offer, and the next day the invention was widely reported in the press.

From that point, there were considerable debates about both the possible medical dangers of tub-bathing and whether taxes should be levied on the household installation of bathtubs. Not many common folk took notice until 1850, when President Millard Fillmore, who had seen the tub when he visited Cincinnati, decided to have one placed in the White House, where it faithfully served executive privilege until Grover Cleveland's presidency.

Well, it was a wonderful story and oddly one of pride to Cincinnatians in the years following 1917, their gullibility notwithstanding. As the nongullible suspected, the entire story was a hoax, revealed as such by Mencken himself in 1926. He was, he admitted, trying to have a bit of fun during the war years and didn't anticipate that the story would be believed and spread to all points emanating from the Queen City.

Is there a distinctive Cincinnati connection to a presidential bathtub? The ghost of William Howard Taft is raised, Cincinnati born and bred and an early dean of the UC law school, the twenty-seventh president of the United States and a chief justice of the U.S. Supreme Court. There is a tale of the tubby Taft stuck in a tub that could not quite accommodate his large frame. The large truth about Taft and his bathtub is that while he served as president from 1908 to 1912, Taft had a tub that was seven feet long and three and a half feet wide built by a New Jersey ironworks firm and installed in the White House. In 1909, he had a similar tub installed on the battleship USS *North Carolina*, another one on his private yacht and an even larger tub in his suite at the Hotel Taft, where he lived for a while after his presidency.

But now for a Cincinnati mystery, and it is not a hoax. At one time, the historic Taft home on Auburn Avenue, now a National Park Service site, held such a huge tub in its lower level. It was said to be either a copy or the White House original, but either way, it could accommodate several normal-sized people. When the house was being restored as an historic site, it was administered by a Friends of the Taft group. When the Park Service took over, the tub was no longer there, and its whereabouts are unknown today. So somewhere in this fair Cincinnati land, there is a huge bathtub, the true remnant of our heritage of bathing, satirical journalism notwithstanding.

Beyond the national correspondents chronicling well-scrubbed Cincinnati, there were writers here who had a genuine American following. "Seckatary Hawkins," the creation of Robert F. Schulkers, published eleven novels of his adventurous juvenile character between 1921 and 1932. Schulkers was born across the Ohio River in Covington, Kentucky, and first serialized his fiction in the *Cincinnati Enquirer* before popularity extended the stories to dozens of newspapers nationwide. Seckatary Hawkins was the ringleader of a group of boys who met in their clubhouse beside the river and solved mysteries in books with such titles as *Seckatary Hawkins in Cuba*, *The Gray Ghost* and *Knights of the Square Table*. The books were bestsellers, especially for that demographic of boys who vicariously seek adventure, and even today there are avid collectors of Schulkers's books.

Another writer of juvenile boys' fiction was a Jesuit priest at St. Xavier College (now Xavier University) Francis J. Finn. The rotund Finn, often seen without his clerical collar and dressed in suspenders, checked tie and crushed fedora, began his writing career while on the faculty of Marquette University. By the time he arrived in Cincinnati in 1890, he had published *Tom Playfair*, which became his most famous novel in a string of books intended to morally uplift the American boy. Finn wrote twenty-seven novels in all, and he often said that his books had their beginnings in the stories he told to his charges in Catholic boarding schools. If the boys promised to behave, he told them, he would read to them from Charles Dickens's *Oliver Twist*. Soon he began making up his own stories, and Tom Playfair was born. Once in Cincinnati and teaching at Xavier, Finn's fiction significantly influenced a public school boy. Theodore Moody Berry was a student at Woodward High School, and as a senior he wrote an essay that saw him named the valedictorian of his graduating class. Berry loved the forthrightness and hard work exemplified by Tom Playfair so he took that as his pen name for the essay. That success as valedictorian took him on to the University of Cincinnati as an undergraduate, followed by his enrollment in the UC College of Law. Later, he would become the first African American mayor of Cincinnati and a key figure in civil rights legislation under President Lyndon Johnson.

4

LIBRARIES AND OTHER BOOKISH BUILDINGS

Deep inside Carl Blegen Library on the University of Cincinnati campus, down in the stacks where the cast-iron supports of the bookshelves hold up the terrazzo floors above them, there is a "No Smoking" sign. It is glued to a battered oak door at the end of an aisle in a secured area closed to the public. The sign is affixed completely to the door, and after decades of age and glue bleed-through, it looks like nicotine stains are coursing down the cardboard as if generations of faculty and staff ignored it with their pipes and cigarettes. Perhaps they did, because there was a time when smoking was tolerated nearly everywhere—though certainly not in library stacks, where the construction design is such that if a spark caught a page or a flyleaf or two, those stacks would act like a chimney and send flutters and flames of paper spiraling upward to the top of the building. So no smoking!

Those aisles and shelves in Blegen Library extend from that old door on one end to ceramic block walls on the other end, and the air—that intoxicating aroma of books that makes us addicts of reading—pulsates with the ghostly spirits of research and revelation, the books and manuscripts reaching hundreds of years back in time. And according to legend, at least one of those ghosts has bodily form eight levels above in the rare book room of the library, a place kept dark and cool and packed with stories of one kind or another. Over time, a book becomes the ghosts of many endeavors: the author, the designer, the printer, the binder, the bookseller and that ruling spirit, the reader.

The new Main Library of the University of Cincinnati opened in 1930, and in 1983 it was renamed as Carl Blegen Library. The building is an art deco treasure with its architectural elements illustrating the history of the book and the heritage of education.

Blegen Library opened in 1930, the second library building on campus, succeeding an earlier classically designed structure, the Van Wormer Library. Opposite in appearance and functional layout from the sandstone of Van Wormer, Blegen's limestone, brick and concrete hold to an art deco form, and the architectural designs throughout the building herald the meaning of books and study and learning, all of which are exclusive to each other until someone can light the way and explain them as books take us from angels to dust. But that overall meaning? Who determines the meaning of libraries? The old tried-and-true consideration of libraries is that they function as both cathedral and fortress—they house the treasures wrought by the human mind and hold them precious. They are protected from forces seeking to diminish or destroy them, often with doors and alarms and sometimes gargoyles and grotesques. But the only effective protective force is the human will.

The question is raised: why does a community want a library? More to the point, why does it need a library? And furthermore, what are the particulars of Cincinnati's creation of libraries?

For several decades in the nineteenth century, Cincinnatians tried to prove they had the earliest public library in the state. For the most part led by local publisher, bookseller and collector Robert Clarke, the effort relied on a notice published in the *Western Spy* newspaper on February 13, 1802, that a committee would meet in Griffin Yeatman's tavern: "Such persons as wish for the establishment of a public library in this town are requested to meet at Mr. Yeatman's at 6 o'clock this evening."

A committee was duly appointed at the meeting, and the members devised a subscription list signed by pioneers Jacob Burnet, Martin Baum, Cornelius Sedam and several others to create a public library. The signatories included other prominent men, including the governor of the Northwest Territory, Arthur St. Clair. The time seemed right to them. Since the river town's founding in 1788, settlers brought their baggage of books with them on their journeys down the Ohio River or across wilderness trails, and there was considerable borrowing and sharing of them. There were even the occasional notices placed in the newspapers by book owners asking that individuals who had borrowed their books to kindly return them. Apparently, stronger measures were unknown as there was a lack of curses placed in the books warning the recalcitrant borrower of disasters to befall the person who did not return books in a timely manner. In the Ohio Valley, the implementation of such curses would easily be evident in the form of floods, locusts, fires, desperate illnesses, drought, hail and various violence, any of which carefully placed on a flyleaf might have provided fair warning.

But regarding that first library, nothing more was learned of the effort, and the document the Cincinnatians signed disappeared for years, coming to light again in the 1860s and in the possession of Clarke. In Clarke's view, the document proved that Cincinnati established this early library, though it seemed that it was just as much a case of vying with the settlement of Ames in Athens County, which formed a library in February 1804 and garnered the nicely frontier nickname of the "Coon-skin Library." Dorothy V. Martin, whose 1944 essay in the *Ohio State Archaeological and Historical Quarterly* thoroughly documents the story of this supposed library and notes Robert Clarke's petulance when challenged over the lack of proof in the matter, as well as the entrenched civic boosterism that refused to give up the honor, instead providing a well-grounded historical analysis.[18] But we shouldn't think that Clarke was just a crusty, harrumphing old-timer. In truth, Robert Clarke, the son of Scottish immigrants, was a gentle, well-mannered man who was devoted to books. Outside of his publishing and bookselling business—or a deep part of it, depending on the point of view—Clarke lived in the beautiful suburb of Glendale and amassed a considerable personal library of Americana, travel and exploration and natural history. He looked every bit the part he played as a nineteenth century bookman: long white beard, round face and piercing eyes and the occasional ink-stained fingers. What he saw in libraries and what he brought to Cincinnati's book world was passion for the printed word and a joy in working with books day in and day out.

Robert Clarke wasn't the only Cincinnatian who believed in the power of libraries. Most of the prominent citizens did, in fact, which was a reasonable and civic-minded cause to believe in, and some of them, such as Timothy C. Day, stepped forward. In Day's view, libraries meant knowledge, and if a person could gain knowledge, experience would not only follow but also foster the getting of additional knowledge. And that, he believed, meant freedom. Amid all this getting and learning, Timothy Day took a humorless and strong-willed stand about most things in life. It showed in his appearance. He stood ramrod straight so that no opponent could bowl him over with wind or words. His politics seemed to affect the very lines of his face and to give his eyes a cast that would wither anyone who dared to oppose him. His brow was always furrowed, and his thin lips were either downwardly frowning or in a constant sneer. Day made Abraham Lincoln look handsome by comparison. Born in 1819, the year Cincinnati was formally incorporated, and educated in the city's public schools, Day worked as a printer and engraver, shaping his views through antislavery pamphlets and newspapers. It was this Cincinnati heritage that gave him his perspective, as it did everyone who was raised during those early decades.

Day became an ardent abolitionist and anti-nativist, and the perfect opportunity for expressing those positions was dropped in his lap in 1850. His older brother owned a half-ownership in the *Cincinnati Enquirer*, and at his death, Day purchased his brother's share. For the next two years, before he sold it, Day used the newspaper to promote his opinion that there should be no extension of slavery into the territories and if his chosen political party, the Democrats, couldn't see things his way, he would take a different path. He sold his share of the newspaper in 1852 and decided to see how things were faring in Europe in terms of slavery and the slave trade. Upon his return, Day represented the Democrat Party in Congress in 1854, but he was dissatisfied with the Democratic platform so he left to embrace Lincoln's Republican Party, though he had a subsequent unsuccessful run for office in 1858. With the outbreak of the Civil War, he further aligned himself with Lincoln and his policies, even with an election as a colonel of a local regiment of African American troops. Once the war was over, in increasingly fragile health, Day turned his attention to education and the Ohio Mechanics Institute.

Abolitionist and newspaper publisher Timothy C. Day believed in the power of libraries, so he provided the Ohio Mechanics Institute, founded in 1828, with the means to create a library for its students. That college is now part of the University of Cincinnati's College of Engineering and Applied Science and its library part of the university's library holdings.

Chartered by the State of Ohio in 1828 to train workers for skilled positions in Cincinnati's rapidly expanding industrial economy, the Ohio Mechanics Institute was governed by local business leaders who had a stake in a vocational workforce. The practical aspect of that education, along with regular lectures to uplift and inspire them, greatly appealed to Day. Before his death from tuberculosis in 1869, he endowed a permanent library for OMI. As Day knew the library at the time, it was already an interesting institution, its shelves filled with training manuals, scientific treatises and textbooks on architecture and design. Day's largesse provided the basis for an excellent library of practicality to grow on that collection. However, there was more to the library than that, even before Day's time. Cincinnati businessmen, those directly involved with OMI as well as those who enthusiastically supported such a school in their city, viewed the library as an opportunity for broadening minds beyond the workaday tasks for which the students were trained. And the fabulous industrial expositions that OMI sponsored in the nineteenth century at Music Hall and its neighbor, Exposition Hall, gave a luster to technical innovations embraced by industrialists around the country. The Cincinnati professional men gave additional books to the library—histories, grammars, art volumes, political tomes, philosophy texts and more. Many of these books were ones they had gathered in their travels in America and abroad, so some of these books were in German, French, Spanish and Italian. Of course, many of these books were never studied by the students; lack of time and interest contributed to these volumes holding a dusty residence on the library's shelves. And yet they gave rise to an interesting anecdote concerning one of America's great inventors.

Thomas Edison arrived in Cincinnati in 1865, working as a telegraph operator. While living in a downtown boardinghouse, Edison found time to attend the shows at the National Theater a few blocks away, but he was also close to OMI and took advantage of the library and its technical holdings. Always fond of his experience there, Edison credited OMI with feeding his hunger for invention. Decades later, probably around the time in 1903 that Edison sent an autographed photo to OMI in response to the school's invitation to attend its seventy-fifth anniversary gala, the story arose that during his stint in Cincinnati, Edison read every book in the OMI library over the course of a single year. It's a great story with the making of a great legend, but like many legends, it had the undisputable core of an impossible quest. Had Thomas Edison actually read all the books in the Ohio Mechanics Institute's library at that time, he would have

Founded in 1835, the Mercantile Library of Cincinnati on Walnut Street is the city's literary center, hosting discussion groups, author talks and anything associated with the love of books and literature.

had to page through nine books a day for a solid year—and be able to read in several languages.

And during these decades, other major libraries in Cincinnati were designed and established. In 1835, the Young Men's Mercantile Library Association of Cincinnati, Ohio—quite a mouthful even then so let's just call it by it's modern name of the Mercantile Library (and in our minds, throw in "the venerable" because it truly is that)—was founded by forty-five young men, some, no doubt, of the common and persistent character noted at the time for a successful mercantile library and essentially young men on the rise in life. In its constitution, those founders stated that they were

> *desirous to adopt the most efficient means to facilitate mutual discourse; to extend our information upon mercantile and other subjects of general utility; promote a spirit of useful inquiry, and qualify ourselves to discharge with dignity the duties or our profession and the social offices of life; have associated ourselves for the purpose of establishing a Library and Reading Room, to be appropriated to the use of young men engaged solely in mercantile pursuits.*[19]

Located in an 1820 Greek Revival building on Fourth Street across from Lytle Park, the Cincinnati Literary Club was founded in 1849. With the motto "Here comes one with a paper" from Shakespeare's *Love's Labour's Lost*, the club's members regularly present papers on topics outside their professions. And those members have always been limited to one hundred in number and always men—a point of contention over the past several years.

Today that reference to "young men" does not hold true. Women are a vital part of the Mercantile Library and have been for many decades. As an aside, that is not the case of another old Cincinnati literary institution, the Literary Club of Cincinnati, founded a decade and a half after the Mercantile Library in 1849.[20] Located on Fourth Street across from Lytle Park in a Greek Revival house built in 1820, the Literary Club is limited to one hundred men, all of whom have come from the professional ranks and whose initial membership is through nomination and election. The men gather for their meetings on Monday evenings during fall, winter and spring, during which one of them will read a paper on a topic of personal interest to the reader in some way and not directly tied to his profession. With membership numbering one hundred, a member can expect to read a paper approximately every two years. And to give the presentations a literary spin, painted on the wall behind the speaker is a quote from Shakespeare's *Love's Labour's Lost*, Act IV, Scene 3: "Here comes one with a paper." It's a nice sentiment, taken out of context as most expressions of quotes from Shakespeare are, but for a genteel anachronism like the

Literary Club, it's part of the charm. The male-only membership rule has come under fire from within and without the club in recent decades, and it caused quite a kerfuffle a few years ago among the members. But the old guard stalwartly stood against the times with an odd concession that wives may attend on the evenings that their husbands read their papers. Here comes one with a paper and his missus.

To return to the subject of the Mercantile Library, as it thrived in the nineteenth century as a library and gathering place for lectures and readings, it was forced to move its location a time or two until it found its current home on Walnut Street, high above Cincinnati's downtown. It will be there forever; in the 1849 lease artfully drawn by Alphonso Taft, lawyer, diplomat, cabinet member under Ulysses Grant, father of William Howard Taft and Mercantile Library member, the library enjoys a ten-thousand-year lease that is perpetually renewable. It is rightfully called the literary center of Cincinnati because of its dynamic membership, book programs and lectures.

Not long after the establishment of the Mercantile Library, the Public Library of Cincinnati and Hamilton County dates its formation to the Ohio Common Schools Act of 1853 that fostered the creation of community libraries in the state. It is now one of the top circulating libraries in the country, with the wide variety of services now incumbent on municipal libraries to serve their citizens, everything from job and grant assistance to homework help and community forums. Not lost in any of this and still of primary purpose is the written word in whatever medium it is conveyed. There aren't many people who remember the grand building that once housed the main branch of the library downtown before its demolition in 1955. Part of that structure on Vine Street was built in 1868, and the plan was for it to be an opera house. But Truman Handy, the man behind the theater, was unable to finish it so the board of education purchased the part that was completed—the front—and the lot behind it. By 1874, the library was completed after an initial opening in 1871, with soaring wrought-iron stairs and stacks, five tiers of alcoves and a grand entrance. The entrance was topped with busts of Benjamin Franklin, William Shakespeare and John Milton.

This was a grand library in every sense of the word. It was architecturally imposing and inspirational to the reader and conveyed the sense of importance Cincinnatians attached to books and reading. The public library system would grow to include deposit stations throughout the city and bookmobiles to serve those not within a practical distance to the library. Later, Cincinnati built nine branch libraries with funds provided by the

PUBLIC
LIBRARY
CINCINNATI ENQUIRER
UNION

Opposite and above: Established in 1853, the Public Library of Cincinnati and Hamilton County moved in 1874 into a beautiful building on Vine Street originally constructed as an opera house. By the 1950s, this structure was woefully inadequate, and by 1955, the library had a new home in a modernist building.

Carnegie Foundation as part of industrialist Andrew Carnegie's efforts to provide access to books throughout the English-speaking world. The Carnegie program was not without controversy. Andrew Carnegie often was seen in the press and by working-class citizens as a brutal captain of industry in how he harshly treated employees in the steel industry he dominated and their labor unions. It was money built on the backs of workers, and some cities were reluctant to accept the funds and mandates of the Carnegie Foundation to build their libraries. Cities also wanted to see the main branch of their public library as a signature grand building in the same way that train stations, post offices, luxury hotels, city halls and ballparks were viewed. The thinking was that these buildings should represent the commercial and philanthropic strength of a city, so grand and distinctive architecture was required. And while some main municipal libraries had Carnegie funds that revealed this approach, for the most part Carnegie libraries were built under a set of rather simple architectural options that worked for rather confined spaces in a neighborhood environment. To receive the funds for construction, the community had to provide the property and the tax base to sustain the library.[21]

For Cincinnati, it was a matter of effectively extending library services and collections throughout the city and county. The nine branch libraries were built between 1905 and 1915 at a total cost of $280,000. Various architects received the commissions to build the libraries, so there were, in fact, some aesthetic variations. The first Carnegie branch in Cincinnati was the Walnut Hills library that opened in 1906, and the last was the West End in 1914. Remarkably, seven of the nine libraries still function as libraries, and an eighth, the Columbia-Tusculum, or East End, branch is now a community arts center. The only branch demolished was the last one constructed, the West End branch, which was torn down in 1947 when it was replaced by a larger branch closer to the center of the neighborhood.

In those various architectural designs of the Cincinnati Carnegies, the Avondale branch on Reading Road is exceptionally beautiful. Designed by the local architectural firm of Frederick W. Garber and Clifford B. Woodward and completed in 1913, it is in a modified Spanish Colonial style. Both Garber and Woodward primarily worked in the Beaux-Arts tradition, but for the Avondale library, they designed an interior of beautiful oak woodwork with a large fireplace and did the roof of the library in red tile. The domed entrance is decorated with Cincinnati's Rookwood tiles. What this library really says of literary heritage comes across through the numerous terra-cotta names of famous authors throughout the ages,

An early bookmobile of the public library system, extending book services outward to neighborhoods and the rest of Hamilton County.

making the entrance act as inspiration for the treasures a reader discovers in the stacks inside.

It was Garber's architect son, Woodie, who would take a severe left turn from his father's style to design the new main library building that opened in 1955.[22] Woodie Garber embraced Modernist architectural design, not an easy aesthetic to sell at the time in Cincinnati. When it came to building design, a conservative point of view definitely held sway. That grand old downtown library had to come down because it could no longer accommodate the growing collections, which required a cleaner and more accessible space. Woodie Garber's vision was for a clutter-free, open space with a soaring atrium. He developed a minimalist design of brick and glass, and from the outside of the building, it has that look and is somewhat forbidding to consider. Once inside, though, Garber's vision is revealed for the innovation he showed in his Modernist point of view. The book stacks and interior courtyard are functional and convey a democratic approach to their design, an approach accessible to anyone. Today, the library at Eighth and Vine Streets has been expanded with a pedestrian bridge to a new component building on Ninth Street that is matched in aesthetics, but the whole effect of the Modernist architecture is softened with the Michael Frasca–designed book fountain at the entrance. Traditionally, library architecture has exhibited a "purpose" function in its design—that is, on the exterior there will be elements that speak of the books that are inside. The Avondale branch library is an excellent example of that. The book fountain balances the clean starkness of Garber's design essentially to say what the building is "about."

There are two other significant twentieth-century buildings in Cincinnati that speak of the heritage of books and reading, structures that once focused on the newspaper trade. The Cincinnati Times-Star building on Broadway Street and the old Cincinnati Enquirer building on Vine Street both have decorative details that illustrate their functions in journalism and printing. The fourteen-story Enquirer Building was designed by Lockwood Greene and Company and opened in 1926 at 617 Vine Street. The newspaper, which had its first issue in 1840, was published at this same site since 1866. It is constructed mainly of limestone so it could accommodate the editorial offices as well as the printing plant.

It is the decorative details in the recessed entrance that are noteworthy. In bronze are several figures that take an art deco approach to the history of printing. There are scribes holding quills and scrolls, a typesetter, a layout editor and a printer with a printing press, all of whom look like an amalgamation of medieval monks with contemporary pressmen and editors. Then there are the limestone figures, again in an art deco interpretation but resembling the gargoyles or grotesques that might be found on the cornices of gothic buildings. Again, there is a scribe, a pressman and a printer. There is also a reader, a figure holding the representation of a newspaper in his hands. The building is one of those whose features are not noticed in passing by on the sidewalk, but a pedestrian who takes a moment to pause can understand the strong connection between past and present in Cincinnati's readers. The Enquirer Building was placed in the National Register of Historic Places in 1975 to acknowledge both its architecture and its heritage of the everyday printed word. A few years later, in 1979, the newspaper's printing facilities moved to the West End, and in 1992 the editorial offices moved to Elm Street. The building was divided into two boutique hotels in 2015.

The Times-Star Building across town at 800 Broadway is also listed in the National Register of Historic Places, earning that distinction in 1983 and for the same reasons as the Enquirer Building. It is another example of art deco architecture illustrating the heritage of printing. It was designed by Samuel Hannaford & Sons of Cincinnati and built in 1933 when the newspaper moved from its former building at Sixth and Walnut

Right: Bronze detail of a reading monk on the former Cincinnati Enquirer Building on Vine Street.

Below: The composing room of the *Cincinnati Times-Star* in 1918.

Left: Sculptural detail of a printer on the art deco former Times-Star Building on Broadway Street.

Right: A bas-relief of fifteenth-century printer William Caxton, one of several printer sculptures on the former Times-Star Building at 800 Broadway. The building now houses Hamilton County offices and the juvenile court.

Streets. The *Cincinnati Times-Star* published from 1880 to 1958 and was an afternoon daily newspaper before it was purchased by another afternoon paper, the *Cincinnati Post* (which ceased publication in 2007). As designed for the newspaper, the building had fifteen stories and took a classical, albeit art deco–inspired, look at the heritage of printing and publishing. On the exterior are reliefs of the notable printers from the 1400s to the 1700s, the likes of Johannes Gutenberg of Germany, William Caxton of England, Robert Estienne of France, the Elzevir family of printers in Holland, Benjamin Franklin of America and Aldus Manutius of Venice. In smaller metallic relief and classically adorned in togas of a sort are printers, typesetters and readers. The lobby inside the building holds beautiful small stainless-steel printers' marks, or trademarks, of the early printers, reproduced along the wall. There are Aldus Manutius again, who printed in the early 1500s, with his distinctive dolphin-and-anchor design

In the library, now resource center, of Hughes High School a sunburst stained-glass window represents a book ornament used by seventeenth-century English bookseller John Partridge.

(meaning "make haste slowly" or do steady and reliable work) and Giovanni Paoli, the first printer in the Americas when he established his press in Mexico City in 1539 and adopted a printer's mark showing a cattle skull. There are also Theodoric Martens, Berthold Rembolt, Christophe Plantin and the unknown printer of St. Albans with their individual devices.

After the *Cincinnati Post* moved to newer quarters in the late 1980s, the Hamilton County Commission bought the building to house juvenile court and judges' offices.

The decorative use of printer's marks may also be seen in Hughes High School, the second-oldest public high school in Cincinnati. Named for Thomas Hughes, a cobbler who wished the city to educate the poor and so bequeathed his property to Cincinnati for that purpose, the first Hughes school was built in 1853 at Fifth and Mound Streets downtown. In 1910, a new Hughes High School was built in University Heights at Clifton and

Calhoun Streets near the University of Cincinnati. Its current name is Hughes STEM High School, and the building is in the Tudor Revival style, complete with a 425-foot tower. On the exterior are grotesques and gargoyles representing the various academic disciplines such as geography, chemistry, art and history. And though the library is now termed a "resource center" and not many books are there, inside that room are exquisite stained-glass windows, twelve of them facing the sunrise in the east, with printer's marks that have been carefully restored.

But the paragon of book architecture in Cincinnati is Blegen Library, with the overall design by local architect Harry Hake. Lee Lawrie, a nationally known sculptor whose work can also be seen in the Los Angeles Public Library; the state capitol in Lincoln, Nebraska; and on Rockefeller Center in New York City, designed the strong, stark faces on Blegen Library that signify the light of knowledge. University of Cincinnati faculty member Ernest Bruce Haswell contributed reliefs on the passing of knowledge from generation to generation and through the centuries. The building is an interesting conglomeration of styles, all adhering to an overall art deco sensibility but with an individualism that contributes to the symmetry of the entire building. When it was designed, faculty from several different disciplines contributed their ideas and opinions, a rare congenial approach to a university project.

Home to three of the twelve libraries at the University of Cincinnati, the Archives & Rare Books Library, the Albino Gorno Memorial Music Library and the John Miller Burnam Classical Library, with its distinctive celebration of heritage of knowledge in its design, Blegen is a hallmark of acknowledging the importance of education and the printed word. There are concrete and limestone reliefs, bronze reliefs and grills and bronze printer's marks and chandeliers with proverbs in different languages that are all about learning. And everything means something important, even the sun disk over the entrance. Atop the words, "The University Library," the disk indicates the blazing light of knowledge. On either side of it are two faces: Phospher, the morning star that celebrates Eastern civilization, and Hesper, the evening star doing the same for Western civilization.

On both the exterior and interior of the library are several representations of owls, their intent being to symbolize learning and wisdom. Many cultures view owls as birds of darkness in their mythology and literature, but when they are regarded as symbolic of education, they're also a symbol of seeking out the light of knowledge.

Above: One of the bronze sculptures on Blegen Library shows the beginnings of writing through hieroglyphics.

Right: Inside the lobby of Blegen Library is a bronze rendition of the famous dolphin and anchor mark of fifteenth-century Venetian printer Aldus Manutius. The Aldine symbol means "make haste slowly."

In the lobby of the building and carried further to the sixth floor are magnificent bronze chandeliers, each of them silhouetted with a proverb about education in different languages. Just inside the lobby is a Japanese proverb, "There are no age limits to learning. Anyone can learn anything if he studies it a hundred times." A few feet beyond this are Egyptian hieroglyphs that read, "Be not proud because of thy knowledge; be not puffed up because of thy manual skill; no art can be wholly mastered; no man can attain perfection in manual skill." The sixth floor was once the main reading room for the library with several chandeliers. There is a Hebrew inscription that takes the words from the Book of Proverbs 3:13, "Happy is the man that findeth wisdom and the man that getteth understanding," and the center lights with the sentiment in Latin from the Roman playwright Terence: "Humani nihil a me alienum puto," or, "Nothing human do I consider alien to myself." Completing the chandeliers in that room is a third one in Greek from philosopher Democritus: "Do not aim at knowing everything."

But the most favored one is found in a side room on the sixth floor. Hanging above the bookshelves is a proverb that is said to have been provided to the architect by a Chinese graduate student in the late 1920s: "Libraries are valuable to readers because they preserve the riches of the world from which come the beginning of wisdom. Everything in the heavens or upon the earth is for our appreciation."

Throughout the building, too, are more than forty printers' marks of notable publishers in the early days of the printed word. Most of these were taken from the colophons of rare books in the University of Cincinnati's collections, chosen for their historical connections as well as their beauty and variously executed by sculptors in plaster, terra cotta, brass and bronze. While many of them are symbols of the printer's name or philosophy of his print shop, the history behind others is telling: the Fust & Schoeffer mark, for instance, is that of Johannes Gutenberg's assistant and the financier who took over his press when Gutenberg could not pay his bills. Fust & Schoeffer completed the printing of Gutenberg's magnificent Bible in the fifteenth century. Or that of Lucantonio Giunta, who died in 1538. As an engraver, printer and publisher, Giunta established print shops throughout Europe, and his design pays homage to his birthplace of Florence. The Florentine *giglio*, or flower, became the city's official symbol in 1250, and Giunta incorporated it into his printer's device. The symbol is ubiquitous throughout Florence. And the device of the French printer Robert Estienne in the sixteenth century shows an olive tree with broken branches, symbolizing the location of his Paris shop at the "sign of the olive." Estienne was so exacting in his typography and printing that he would take his proof sheets and hang them outside his shop, offering a reward to anyone who could find a mistake in his work. Unfortunately, Estienne eventually ran afoul of the Inquisition doctors at the Sorbonne who disagreed with how he was interpreting some of his Bible work. So in order to avoid being roasted at the stake, Estienne lit out for Switzerland and spent the rest of his life there.

There is one particular symbol on the building, however, that seems to define not only the heritage of knowledge, but the purpose of education and community responsibility as well. An ouroboros is located in the window grille on the southwest side of the library. This design motif is small and unnoticed unless you look very closely, and the green patina has rendered the symbol difficult to trace with the eye. It is an ancient concept, that of a serpent swallowing its own tail. In this age-old symbol that can be traced as far in the past as a fourteenth century BCE Egyptian funeral text, the ouroboros signifies the cycle of life and death as well as the constant return of magic and knowledge in each generation.

The symbol rests with more than the ancient Egyptian netherworld, though its influence moved to Greek magic and, eventually, Western medieval alchemy. Some element of the ouroboros is found in cultures throughout the world. In Scandinavian mythology for example, the serpent is a child of the god Loki that encircles the world. For Amazonian cultures, the snake latching on to its own tail is a symbol of the world and its creation. In India, it is Kundalini, representing divine power. Even in contemporary folklore, there is a touch of the ouroboros: in Appalachia folklore there is an old belief told that a black snake or a king snake could grab its tail in its mouth and roll downhill. If you ever saw it, you were forbidden to stop its path because if the snake released its tail, our memories would be lost and the world might end. There is a similarity in this tale with mythologist Joseph Campbell's analysis of the serpent as an archetype of creative energy and cosmic generation of knowledge. So is this part of a library's purpose?

These characteristics of the ouroboros—eternal knowledge, the circle of life, the beginning and end of time and existence, the notion of duality, the idea of giving and receiving of knowledge—fits in well with all the other decorative architectural elements of Blegen Library. The intent of this art is to inspire students and faculty to be an integral part of education and learning and imbue us with the responsibility of discovery and of sharing knowledge.

And within the circled serpent is a shield with these words: "Quod Tibi Fieri Non Vis Alteri Ne Peceris." There is a slight mistake by the sculptor here, Peceris should be Feceris, the basic translation being "Do Unto Others As You Would Have Done Unto You." And like the ouroboros, this sentiment is also found in cultures throughout the world. So in its own way, Blegen Library in its design and function is an expression of global life, civic engagement and world knowledge.

5

FOR THE LOVE OF SHAKESPEARE

On June 20, 2020, Letha Jane Greene of Cincinnati died at the age of seventy-seven. Greene was the descendant of a prominent family of steamboat captains on the Ohio River and spent a fair amount of her childhood riding on the *Delta Queen*, the *Mississippi Queen* and other historic paddle wheelers, but she made her own mark in the classroom. Jane Greene was a high school English teacher in love with Shakespeare. After earning degrees from the University of Cincinnati and Xavier University, Greene taught for thirty-two years at Withrow High School, the same high school from which she graduated. In her teaching of Shakespeare, she had her students stage a funeral for the conflicted and melancholy Hamlet, complete with hymns, a eulogy and press coverage. When she taught *Julius Caesar*, Greene stirred the students' interest by offering a cash prize to the first one who greeted her on March 15 with "Beware the Ides of March!" In her life and in her teaching, Letha Jane Greene reflected a two-hundred-year tradition of Cincinnati embracing the Bard.

That affection for Shakespeare's words in Greene's life is part of a heritage that began almost at the same moment that soldiers and settlers descended on the land along the Ohio River that became Cincinnati. The soldiers in Fort Washington put on various plays to entertain themselves, mainly the farces and comedies of the time, but occasionally a soliloquy of Shakespeare's was recited as well or lines from *Macbeth* or *Othello* were presented to an audience drawn from the garrison. The situation was the same when more and more people established themselves in Cincinnati, and when it grew enough to be a real city in the nineteenth century, Cincinnati was like several other cities in frontier America with Shakespeare recited both on the stage and in home parlors. Along with the growing cities in the Northwest Territory and up and down the Ohio River and down into the South, Cincinnati was on the general circuit tours that included Pittsburgh, Louisville, St. Louis, Savannah, Charleston, Mobile and New Orleans. Acting troupes traveled by flatboat to stop in Cincinnati, and by the late 1830s this river highway was complemented by overland travel by stagecoach. These groups of performers were led by managers and impresarios like Samuel Drake (whose company included nearly all his family members) and N.M. Ludlow, who wrote about those early days in his 1880 memoir, *Dramatic Life As I Found It*: "I started on horseback for Cincinnati with Mr. Phillips as my coadjutor. We made the journey in about seven days; riding early and late, stopping only two hours in the middle of the day, to feed our horses, eat our dinners, and rest a little."[23]

Ludlow's visit was in 1817, and he found a theatrical group already here, that of a Billy Turner, whose mismanagement caused the actors to forego their salaries, leading to complaints and insubordination. Ludlow didn't think much of Cincinnati. At the time, he said, it had about eight thousand inhabitants and should have been a better town for theater, but it didn't rise to the enthusiasm of Nashville or Louisville. Even at that time, it was said that Cincinnati's first theater was established in 1801, and there were regular visits by 1815, but it wasn't really until 1820 that an actual theater was constructed, the Columbia Street Theater. That theater was followed by more and more theaters, some lasting just a few years and others finding success for decades. Light comedies and standard Shakespearean fare as *King Lear*, *Hamlet*, *Romeo and Juliet*, *Richard III* and *Macbeth* were the most popular offerings.

One of the earliest actors with a national reputation to play in Cincinnati was Thomas Abthorpe Cooper, an English tragedian on tour in America. He came to Cincinnati to play Othello, a production that on one night became a comedy. It seems a young lady came late to the performance, arriving just at the part of the play when Othello speaks to the senators and the Duke of Venice. The woman looked about for a seat, unable to find one until she noticed several unoccupied chairs on the stage. A bit confused in her own whereabouts and unfamiliar with Shakespeare or the play, she decided to sit in one of those empty chairs. Cooper happened to be turned in her direction and had reached the part of his speech when he says, "Here comes the lady," and the senators partly rose from their seats, anticipating

Othello's wife, Desdemona. The late arrival thought it was all for her but was somewhat embarrassed by the cheers and laughter that greeted her. The amused uproar lasted for several minutes until a kind soul rescued her and directed her to a seat in the audience.

Other reputable actors followed Cooper to Cincinnati, including Thomas Souness Hamblin, a contemporary of Junius Booth Sr., Edwin Forrest and William Macready. In October 1829, Hamblin came to the Columbia Street Theater to give a series of performances in the roles of Hamlet, Macbeth and Brutus. He was a well-known thespian, so the owner of the theater, Samuel Drake (who was among the first to come to Cincinnati by flatboat and set up performances), decided the attraction of Hamblin was worth a raise in ticket prices to the considerable sum of a dollar. The audiences were all-male and rather rowdy, though Hamblin didn't mind the roughness of his audience. Outside of his acting, he was widely known as a saloon brawler, so if he was heckled, he could take care of himself—and he often did.

That behavior was typical of Cincinnati audiences, and there was plenty of catcalls during the performances. If we look at these playgoers with an eye to Shakespeare's day, they were not unlike the groundlings who stood before the stage in the Globe Theatre, occasionally entranced by the actors' words and the play's actions but just as often talkative or jeering. The Cincinnati groundlings perhaps were a bit more respectful of the actresses, especially if they were local performers. One of these actresses was Belinda Groshon, born in London in 1788 but who came to America to build a career on the stage. It isn't known how—or even why—she came to Cincinnati, but by 1820, she had become a fixture in local productions and a favorite of the citizens here. Her signature role was Lady Macbeth, and her fate was Shakespearean to a fault. In 1822, she was performing that part in the new Second Street Theater when she collapsed on stage and died. Presumably, she was buried in one of Cincinnati's cemeteries close to downtown, but the affection for her was such that sometime after Spring Grove Cemetery was founded in 1844 at the northern reaches of the city, her body was removed by her children and reinterred there. Her grave was topped by a life-sized statue, and these words were carved on the base: "This monument is raised as a memorial of filial devotion for departed genius."

From the 1820s through the years of the Civil War, frontier Cincinnati developed an appreciation that varied in tone from the rowdy audiences who sometimes kept more genteel playgoers away to another element that exercised a distinct class difference from the common citizens in their love for Shakespeare. These differences cropped up a number of times.

Local Shakespearean actress Belinda Groshon was on stage in Cincinnati's new theater on Second Street in the winter of 1822 when she suddenly died. She was so beloved by her fellow actors and by her fans that after Spring Grove Cemetery was founded in 1845, a statue of her was installed above her reburial.

In 1827, Englishwoman Frances Trollope came to America with a small entourage to try to rebuild her family's finances. In Cincinnati, she built Trollope's Bazaar, a retail business venture that was as much bizarre as bazaar. It's doubtful that Trollope or her townsmen ever really settled on what it was: in some odd Egyptian-styled building with a Moorish tower, the Bazaar was by turns and at the same time a coffeehouse, dry goods store, lecture hall and theater. As it became known as Trollope's Folly, the enterprise failed, and by 1830, the Trollopes had fled home to England. But while they were here, Frances (better known as "Fanny") tried to find something to jumpstart a career for her overindulged, wastrel son, Henry. Fanny enjoyed giving lavish entertainments, and at one such party she had Henry exhibit his thespian aspirations. He gave a brief performance as John Falstaff in *The Merry Wives of Windsor*, leading one writer to later comment, "Falstaff's good, round belly was found to be lined with sack instead of capon, and the play was incredibly funny, for he was very drunk, and had a small featherbed tucked under his waistcoat." After her return to England, Trollope wrote her account of the years in America, which became a best-seller, and in it she was not shy about expressing her snobbery in Cincinnati. She disliked the theaters and most of the actors, comparing them to the illustrious English actors she had seen in the past, but mostly she abhorred the audiences:

> *An annoyance greater than decorations indifferently clean, was the style and manner of the audience. Men came into the lower tier of boxes without their coats; and I have seen shirt sleeves tucked up to the shoulder; the spitting was incessant, and the mixed smell of onions and whiskey.... The bearing and attitudes of the men are perfectly indescribable; the heels thrown higher than the head, the entire rear of the person presented to the audience, the whole length supported on the benches, are among the varieties that these exquisite posture-masters exhibit. The noises, too, were perpetual, and of the most unpleasant kind; the applause is expressed by cries and thumping with the feet, instead of clapping; and when a patriotic fit seized them, and "Yankee Doodle" was called for, every man seemed to think his reputation as a citizen depended on the noise he made.*[24]

All in all, it seemed the Cincinnati audiences were like Shakespeare's groundlings, only with seats.

But from boots to bottoms, Cincinnati audiences did know the plots of the plays as well as a fair amount of dialogue, this familiarity developed mainly from abridged versions or extracts from the plays. Those class differences exhibited in a classless way by Fanny Trollope were most emphasized with the creation of the Shakespeare Club, initially under the auspices of the elocutionist John Celivergos Zachos, a Constantinople-born Greek who came to the United States in 1830. Zachos was a well-accomplished man who was a physician, inventor, educator and literary scholar. By the 1850s, he was in Ohio advocating educational reform and teaching at Antioch College, where he associated himself with Horace Mann. Zachos's most well-known book was *The Primary School Speaker: A Collection of Pieces, Colloquies, and Dialogues, Designed for Children in Schools From the Ages of Six to Twelve*, published in Cincinnati in 1860. If life was fair, a child could just elocute the long title of the book and call it a day. Later, Zachos would serve as a surgeon during the Civil War and follow that with a career in the ministry. Before all that, however, in the late 1850s, he helped form the Shakespeare Club of Cincinnati. With his long, white patrician beard and definite opinions about nearly everything, including how to recite Shakespeare's lines, he was perfect for the role of leader.

The club was a curious one (they apparently couldn't agree on the spelling, sometimes going with "Shakespeare" and other times with "Shakespere" or even "Shakspere" and couldn't come to consensus on their founding date, either 1859 or 1860), its members drawn from an upwardly mobile middle class. For the most part, Zachos and his fellow Shakespeare lovers felt that excerpts from the plays were best employed both as elocutionary exercises and, in the confines of drawing rooms and the occasional rental of a small theater, as entertainment in high culture. Of course, this point of view was similarly expressed by similar groups in similar cities on the frontier. In the Cincinnati club's perspective, it was necessary to stay above hoi polloi. The members were confident that in their circumscribed performances, which mainly consisted of readings rather than full productions, there would be no spitting, no muddy boots and no hooting. The Shakespeare Club would adjust its ways after 1876, appearing in costume in venues like Melodeon Hall at Fourth and Walnut Streets and Pike's Opera House, also on Fourth Street, between Vine and Walnut, while still shying from the bloody-handed portrayal of Lady Macbeth. Gentler audience members might swoon. One of the club's post-Zachos leaders was Albert W. Whelpley, who acted variously as president, treasurer and Bassonio in *The Merchant of Venice*. Later in his life, Whelpley also served as a member of the Cincinnati Typothetae association of master printers, a bookseller, president of the Ohio Library Association and head of the public library from 1886 to 1900. He obviously led a life devoted to the printed word.

Still, having major Shakespearean productions and famous actors traveling down and up river to Cincinnati—including the likes of William Macready, Edwin Forrest, Junius Booth Sr. (who once ran drunkenly down a Cincinnati street after someone who had crossed him, waving a sword and shouting words often not heard in parlors) and his sons, Junius Jr., Edwin and John Wilkes—continued to hold great favor. During the 1850s and 1860s, John Wilkes Booth was a mainstay on the Cincinnati stage, most often appearing in productions of *Richard III*, *King Lear*, *Macbeth*, *Hamlet* and *Julius Caesar* (and when he was captured and killed after his assassination of Abraham Lincoln, in his wallet was found the photograph of actress Fanny Brown, born in Cincinnati as Fanny McFarland, whose parents were traveling circus performers). Junius Jr., too, often played Cincinnati and in fact was in town performing in April 1865 when news of his brother's crime reached the city. Angry crowds tore down the playbills promoting his appearance in Pike's Opera House, and for his own safety, Junius was spirited out of Cincinnati.

And then there was Edwin Forrest, perhaps the most lauded American Shakespearean actor of the 1840s, but who didn't have such a great decade. His acting rival was the celebrated English thespian William Macready. A feud between the two heated up in 1846 when each actor disparaged the other over his portrayals of Hamlet on stage. Forrest thought Macready's interpretation was effete and overly dramatic. Macready thought Forrest's was done to the effects of American bumpkinism. Their dispute escalated until audiences on both sides of the Atlantic favored one or the other, and the arguments between the factions often came down to a lingering American antagonism against England for taxes and wars past and to a rising nativist sentiment. When Macready was on his American tour in 1848, one of his stops was in Cincinnati. During his performance as Hamlet, a Forrest supporter cast the half carcass of a sheep on to the stage. While we are not sure where the man was sitting, wherever it was required quite the arm strength. The particular meaning of the sheep is lost unless the offended party thought it quite nicely expressed Macready's bleating on stage. As it turned out, others in the audience were more upset with the sheep-pitcher, surrounding him and escorting him out of the theater. The Forrest-Macready feud did not end there. The next year, 1849, saw the infamous Astor Place Riot in New York City, where mobs used the opportunity of the feud to go on a rampage in which twenty-two people were killed and over one hundred injured.

Forrest's 1848 performances in Cincinnati were also marked in a disputatious way. At that time, Forrest was married to a sometime actress and full-time social climber by the name of Catherine Norton Sinclair. By the time they arrived in Cincinnati in May to perform in *Julius Caesar* and other plays, their marriage was already falling apart. On one afternoon, with leisure time before the evening's performance, Forrest decided to step outside the hotel for a short constitutional and perhaps a drink or two in a local saloon. When he returned and entered his hotel room, he found Sinclair in a compromising position with a supporting actor, George Jamieson, who was cast in the play as Brutus. It was all fodder for the lurid revelations in Forrest and Sinclair's divorce trial in 1851. The 1848 incident as presented by Sinclair's attorney was that Forrest walked in on Jamieson conducting a phrenological exam on Sinclair, the study of the characteristics of human skull bumps being very popular at the time. But regarding the person of Jamieson, he died in 1868 when, having missed his train near Yonkers, New York, he was walking back up the line when he was struck by the express train. Little else is known about him other than a few biographical sentences that state his mother was an actress of considerable talent and his father was just an Irishman.

The place of theaters and their audiences in community life continued to be controversial. Even when local abolitionist and firebrand preacher Lyman Beecher railed against the immorality of the theaters, especially evidenced by the notorious "third tier," he was countered by actress and theater manager Olive Logan, who asserted that despite any moral equivocation, theatrical productions had cultural value for the Cincinnati community. Logan began her life as a child actress along with her sister Eliza, under the tutelage of their father, an Irishman by the grand name of Cornelius Ambrosius Logan, who managed several local theaters.

The third tier, common in many cities, was the top level of seating in a theater, notorious as a pick-up spot for prostitutes. The reputation of urban theaters was dicey enough, with ministers and moral reformers campaigning against it in the pulpit and the polling booths. Logan, who grew up in the theatrical world, certainly knew this but contended that the elimination of the third tier would salve the sordid shortcomings of public entertainment. In her memoirs, she wrote about her experiences as an actress and manager:

> *It is within my own recollection that the hideous abomination known as the "third tier" was in inexistence in our theatres....I well remember in early girlhood, having looked up from my place on the stage* [in the 1840s she played the boys' roles in Richard III] *to the brutal exhibition of faces in the gallery, with something such a feeling as one might have in looking over into pandemonium.*[25]

Olive Logan noted, too, that the *Cincinnati Enquirer* waged a campaign against the National Theater, which caused it to close temporarily due to adverse public opinion. As she said, "Reader, think for a moment on the idea of the management. Is it not horrible, revolting, and diabolical?" The National Theater was the last venue in Cincinnati to eliminate the third tier.

But Shakespearean performance was also used to raise money for good causes, which added to its cultural weight. An example was an 1865 Civil War benefit, a performance organized and staged at Pike's Opera House by the very respectable local businessman Enoch Carson, the prominent Mason and Shakespeare bibliophile. In Carson's benefit for the war's widows and orphans, even the lieutenant governor of Ohio, Charles Anderson, took part, playing the role of Hamlet. Carson assumed a small role himself as the first gravedigger. The *Hamlet* benefit included a special prologue by Thomas Buchanan Read, a poet already renowned in the North for his 1864 dramatic poem, "Sheridan's Ride," about the battlefield bravery of General Philip Sheridan. Read was a Cincinnati resident at the time, writing his verse from his residential hotel on Eighth Street. "Sheridan's Ride" had its performance debut in a reading at the Mercantile Library, performed by James E. Murdoch, a famous Shakespearean and elocutionist who had moved to southwest Ohio in 1850.

Born in Philadelphia in 1811, Murdoch first played Hamlet in 1845 at the Park Theater in New York City. The Hamlet role became his signature one, and over the next few decades of his career, he won some acclaim in the United States for his acting, not only for Hamlet but for other Shakespearean roles and the occasional drama as well. But he was equally known for his elocution lectures, as the author of books on the subject, and as a performer of poetry which was as widely applauded as his Shakespeare parts. In particular, during the Civil War his recitation of "Sheridan's Ride" won the favor of audiences throughout the North, including that of President Abraham Lincoln. Quickly spreading throughout the Union states, the narrative poem of seven stanzas celebrates the ride of General Philip Sheridan to the Battle of Cedar Creek and the victory of the Union troops. It concludes:

Hurrah! hurrah for Sheridan!
Hurrah! hurrah for horse and man!
And when their statues are placed on high
Under the dome of the Union sky,
The American soldier's Temple of Fame,
There, with the glorious general's name,
Be it said, in letters both bold and bright:
Here is the steed that saved the day
By carrying Sheridan into the fight,
From Winchester—twenty miles away!

With his many recitations of the verse as demanded by the American public, Murdoch made the poem as famous as his performances in *Hamlet*. Cincinnatians embraced the tragedian as one of them, as he owned a farm in nearby Warren County and resided part of his time within the city limits.

Near his rural home there was even a small settlement called Murdoch with a post office of the same name. Road signs today still indicate Murdoch, long after the post office was discontinued. And there is an active church, Bethel Murdoch Presbyterian, in the area.

To return to that night of Carson's benefit, seats in the theater sold for one and two dollars and the playbill was elaborately printed on silk, an indication of the production's importance in raising money for soldiers' families.

In the years after the war, more public benefits fronted by Shakespeare plays would be offered, including a prominent event by the Shakespeare Club, noted for the rarity of one of its performances open for the general public. During a scourge of yellow fever in 1878, the club gave a testimonial in Robinson's Opera House to the Douglas Division of the Knights of Pythias, with the proceeds donated to the fever's victims.

But the temper of the times was changing. The Cincinnati audiences for Shakespeare, as they were in other cities and in Great Britain, were no longer the rough uncouth playgoers before the Civil War. Shakespeare's plays in Cincinnati life were established entertainment that was generally appreciated by the aspiring middle class as well as the upper class in a burgeoning industrial city with a centralized school system where passages from Shakespeare were required exercises in elocution and oratory and in the teaching of English literature and several solid theaters that offered a wide range of entertainment from high to low, including burlesque shows, low and middlebrow comedies and maudlin drama. Performances of Shakespeare were refined and almost elitist in nature by the 1880s and 1890s. Notable tragedians continued to stop in Cincinnati during their circuit travels, from Charlotte Cushman to Helen Modjeska, Henry Irving (whose manager was Bram Stoker, the author of *Dracula*) and virtually every Shakespearean of note in the American and English theater world. But it would be another century before the Bard's plays would become accessible for everyone again when the Cincinnati Shakespeare Company was founded.

In April 1883, the long anticipated Dramatic Festival of Shakespeare plays in Cincinnati, Ohio, was underway. During a performance of *Julius Caesar* at Music Hall, the players were in the middle of Act III, Scene 1 when Antony sees the dead Caesar and says:

O, pardon me, thou bleeding piece of earth,
That I am meek and gentle with these butchers!
Thou art the ruins of the noblest man
That ever lived in the tide of times.

In that Cincinnati production, the direction called for James E. Murdoch, he of the stentorian voice who read "Sheridan's Ride," as Marc Antony to pull back a sheet covering Caesar's head, Caesar being played by the actor Louis James. However, Murdoch mixed up his stage direction and instead of the face of the murdered man, Antony reveals a pair of very white and hairy feet. The audience had a good laugh as Antony walked to the other end of the bier and pulled back the sheet to uncover James's face.

A few nights later, Murdoch was again on the stage in the festival's production of *Hamlet*. On that night, he performed fairly well as the young Dane, at least to most of the audience's approval, even though he wasn't what most of them expected of an actor playing Hamlet. After all, Murdoch was seventy-two years old. Actress Marie Wainwright, who had just turned thirty, played Ophelia. The Cincinnati audience approved because James Edward Murdoch was one of them.

In 1878, the Music Hall was constructed, designed by Cincinnati's eminent architect, Samuel Hannaford. It would become the performance home for the Cincinnati College of Music concerts, the annual Maifest concerts that grew from the German immigrant population and became the May Festival Chorus, as well as for visiting orchestras and acting troupes. And by 1882, it had become the venue for the Shakespeare festival as conceived by local theater manager and impresario Colonel R.E.J. Miles. The star was James Edward Murdoch.

Miles was a longtime promoter of various entertainments in Cincinnati. His theaters, variously the Grand Opera House and the Robinson Opera House (*opera* being a very loose term here here), presented Shakespeare plays, but they also offered melodramas, comedies and lowbrow fare, sometimes with horses and highwaymen and fire and always with elaborate sets. Much of his offerings could be considered pre-vaudevillian. The Colonel, as he styled himself, embraced the notion of extravaganza in everything he undertook. And in 1883, when his hired director for the Shakespeare plays was for various reasons unavailable for a time, Miles decided to direct rehearsals himself. The sets on the massive Music Hall stage would be spectacular and unforgettable for audience and the backdrops the most visually arresting that had ever accompanied a Shakespeare play. At least in his mind, and given his temperament and tastes, it was no surprise that at one point the artists hired to do the sets and backdrops went on strike.

The labor dispute was soon settled, and Miles proceeded with his plans for a remarkable event. The promotional items and cardboard souvenirs played about with the Shakespeare image, and Miles published lengthy programs that included scenes from the plays so the audience could read along with the dialogue on the stage. In advertising, he featured the eminent actors he hired for the weeklong event, performers of considerable national repute such as Murdoch, of course, and Mary Anderson, Lawrence Barrett, Clara Morris, Nat Goodwin, Hortense Rhea, Otis Skinner, Louis James and many others, who took the roles in *Julius Caesar*, *Romeo and Juliet*, *Hamlet* and *Much Ado About Nothing*. Even John McCullough was featured, already in the final throes of the syphilis that would see him break down at Chicago's McVicker's Theater the next year, taking him from his distinguished career to a death in a Philadelphia asylum in 1885. He took on one of his strongest roles in *Othello*.

And James E. Murdoch, in his dotage, played the young Hamlet.

Once underway during the last days of April in 1883 and extending into the first week of May, the grand Music Hall next to the Miami-Erie Canal bisecting the urban blocks was the focus of the entire city. The festival was attended by thousands and covered by journalists from *Puck*, *Harper's Weekly* and national newspapers such as the *New York Times* as well as the several hometown papers. The critics were enthusiastic—even toward a seventy-two-year-old Hamlet—and while *Puck* lampooned all the hoopla, as was its editorial bent, the other journals and papers were enthusiastic in their

A souvenir from the 1883 Cincinnati Dramatic Festival that featured several well-known actors appearing at Music Hall in Shakespeare's plays.

accounts and, in the case of *Harper's*, carried the engravings of the actors, the theater interior and the backstage costumes and props.

Those thousands of playgoers reflected the middle and upper classes who either knew Shakespeare from performances in earlier years or who loved the thrill of a festival, and tens of thousands more read the details of each performance the next day in the dailies. What was happening in the nightly productions was the setting of an expectation for Shakespeare acting and presentation. The expectation was that Shakespeare was worth commemorating in an elaborate fashion. Though many of the actors in the festival were familiar to Cincinnatians because of previous appearances here, it was seeing them on the stage of the magnificent Music Hall rather than in the theaters that led to a notion that Shakespeare could be more than an evening on the town; it could be a major and memorable event. This staging of the plays developed a local sense of how to approach Shakespeare in acting technique, set design and theater management that governed the city's style over the next generation, even to Cincinnati's celebration of the Shakespeare Tercentenary in 1916. The 1883 festival determined in large measure how local theater lovers understood and appreciated the plays because of the intense experience of a night-after-night festival and the heavy coverage in the newspapers. The festival substantially colored their views of a high-toned experience that was available to them. It also established a cultural value that could be perpetuated for the future. (We would expect that given the Victorian adoration of Shakespeare in England and America, Cincinnatians would wish to permanently commemorate him in the manner of other cities with a statue perhaps, or a formal garden. This did not prove to be the case. As an aside, even today Cincinnati has relatively few statues, especially of individuals.)

However, the love of Hamlet—or at least the actor who portrayed him and the extravagant stage backdrop that supported him—led to a real monument. *Hamlet* was performed on Friday, May 4. The story, as reported in the newspaper, was that one of the attendees for that performance was the superintendent of the Cincinnati Water Works, a Mr. A.G. Moore. Sitting in the audience with the thousands of other citizens, Moore was rather taken with the painting of Elsinore Castle that was the stage set. It was a backdrop that measured sixty-five feet by sixty-five feet and apparently was a beautifully rendered image of a castle somewhere in the world and somewhere in the imagination. What particular castle is anyone's guess, then or now—a newspaper illustration provided a glimpse of what the backdrop looked like. At any rate, at this point in 1883, Moore was charged with building a valve house for the water supply tunnel that extended from the reservoir in Eden Park down to Gilbert Avenue at the foot of the Mount Adams neighborhood. This park and reservoir were on the east side of the city, completely across town from Music Hall. Although the vision for the valve house was as a workaday functional structure, Moore had the idea that it could be a physical monument in tribute to the play he saw showcased at the festival. So on the following Monday, May 7, Moore met with several architects, and the one who earned the commission—one Charles Hannaford, son of the aforementioned Samuel who designed Music Hall—submitted a design that looked like a castle in a Norman Romanesque Revival style, and it was called "Elsinore Tower" or "Elsinore Arch." The plaque on the arch simply says "Elsinore, A.D. 1883." Though Shakespeare never really described his Elsinore to any degree, the Cincinnati Elsinore bore—and bears—no resemblance to Kronborg Castle in Helsingor, Denmark, the historical inspiration for Shakespeare. With this construction for the waterworks, the city acknowledged the place of Shakespeare in its culture, and a few years later, in 1893, a photograph of the arch was included in an expensive coffee table–style book that illustrated Cincinnati's prominent buildings. Elsinore still stands in Cincinnati and is recognized as part of its architectural heritage. In 1980, it was listed in the National Register of Historic Places.

As for commemorating the aging Murdoch's performance, when he died ten years later, his friends and fans commissioned a grand marble bust of him to be exhibited in the public library. As mentioned before, that library was housed in a building originally intended as an opera house but never used as such, and Murdoch's bust was placed on a marble pedestal in the lobby of the finished library. Today, with that library building demolished in 1955 and the current postmodern structure in its place, the Murdoch bust rests in the basement, securely tied down so its massive weight cannot cause it to fall over. Murdoch himself is buried in Spring Grove Cemetery, his epitaph from Act I, Scene 2 of *Hamlet* when the young Hamlet speaks of his father: "He was a man, take him for all in all. I shall not look upon his like again."

The next year, 1884, another dramatic festival was held, also successful in both audience favor and at the box office, but Colonel Miles the ever-ambitious impresario had moved on to other thespian spectacles. The stage was solidly set for the future, however. Music Hall became the main—in fact, for many years the only—venue for festival-like drama productions. Cincinnatians had a notion that while regular Shakespeare productions

After the tremendous success of the 1883 festival, the love for the Bard extended to the architectural design for a Cincinnati Waterworks pumping station at the foot of Eden Park. *Hamlet* lived on in "Elsinore Castle."

were fine, they were capable of celebrating and performing his plays as a cultural mark for the city.

Just a few short years before Cincinnati's dramatic festivals, local photographer James Landy created his own tribute to the words of Shakespeare.[26] Landy's inspiration was one of the most famous lines in literature: "All the world's a stage, and all the men and women merely players," Shakespeare's words from *As You Like It*, Act II, Scene 7, as they are spoken by his character, Jacques, a morose and melancholy man. As part of Jacques's speech, the line is so often invoked about life in the theater, about everyday life and about everyone's cosmic role in an earthly existence that we almost expect to see it carved on public buildings and scribbled on alley walls, and perhaps it is somewhere in some place. Beyond that opening line, however, is a poem that describes the path from the cradle to the grave and what we experience along the way from birth to oblivion:

They have their exits and their entrances,
And one man in his time plays many parts,
His acts being seven ages. At first, the infant,
Mewling and puking in the nurse's arms.
Then the whining schoolboy, with his satchel
And shining morning face, creeping like snail
Unwillingly to school. And then the lover,

Sighing like furnace, with a woeful ballad
Made to his mistress' eyebrow. Then a soldier,
Full of strange oaths and bearded like the pard,
Jealous in honour, sudden and quick in quarrel,
Seeking the bubble reputation
Even in the cannon's mouth. And then the justice,
In fair round belly with good capon lined,
With eyes severe and beard of formal cut,
Full of wise saws and modern instances;
And so he plays his part. The sixth age shifts
Into the lean and slippered pantaloons,
With spectacles on nose and pouch on side;
His youthful hose, well saved, a world too wide
For his shrunk shank, and his big manly voice,
Turning again toward childish treble, pipes
And whistles in his sound. Last scene of all,
That ends this strange eventful history,
Is second childishness and mere oblivion,
Sans teeth, sans eyes, sans taste, sans everything.

William Shakespeare, being Shakespeare, took an ancient notion of dividing human existence into stages or eras, a popular motif in both literature and art, and put to it his own writing talent, even using the concept in more than one play. In much of his work, Shakespeare borrowed, refined, refreshed, created anew and made stories and lines immortal. Even the idea of life as a stage and men and women merely players playing a part extended at least to the Roman poet Juvenal in the first century, who used it to describe Greece and Greeks in *Satire 3*.

Those "seven ages" of man penned by William Shakespeare in *As You Like It* became a popular theme in the nineteenth century, when there was a virtual mania for anything about the Bard—editions of his plays for both children and adults, etchings of his characters and stage settings, statues and commemorative collectibles. There were various literary takes on the subject as well as paintings, tableaus and photographic interpretations. One of the most celebrated sets of pictures were the ones made in 1876 by Landy. He created them for a showing at the Centennial Exhibition in Philadelphia that year, presenting them in three formats: a set of small cabinet cards, or cartes de visite, a set of large prints and as a book with tipped-in photographs, published in Cincinnati the next year by Robert

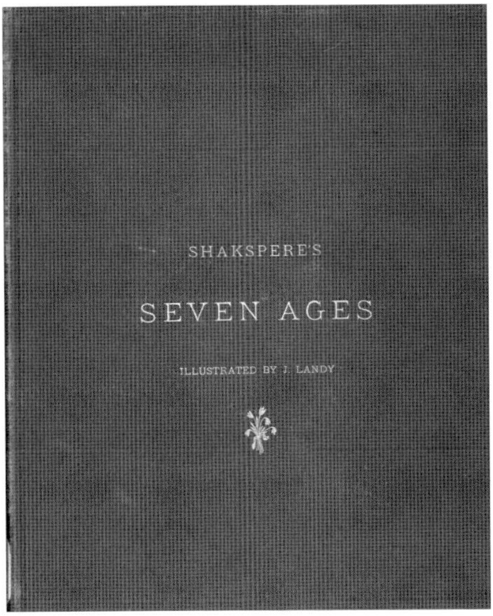

One of Cincinnati's most eminent photographers in the nineteenth century, James Landy often took photos of the numerous visiting Shakespearean actors and actresses for their promotional cartes de visite. In 1876 he published his own take on Shakespeare, using the famous "Seven Ages of Man" from *As You Like It.*

Clarke's publishing company. Landy's book is formally titled *Shakespere's Seven Ages of Man, Illustrated with Photographs from Life.* As was the case with Cincinnati's Shakespeare club, the spelling of Shakespeare was interchangeable with what is the accepted spelling today.

As a photographer, James Landy was very familiar with the passion for Shakespeare. He was born in New York City in 1838, and at the age of twelve, he began his career by working as an apprentice in the photography studio of Silas Holmes on Broadway. He came to Cincinnati in 1862 during the Civil War and set up a studio on Fourth Street just opposite Pike's Opera House, which regularly presented Shakespeare plays. Often the touring actors went to Landy's studio to have their pictures taken for promotional photo cards. Though in the early days of his career he made daguerreotypes, when that technology was supplanted by collodion photography, he employed that. By the 1870s, he was using the dry-plate or gelatin emulsion process. Of course, Landy photographed more than Shakespeareans. He was noted as well for his photographs of many celebrities and politicians, as well as for his pictures of buildings, scenes, the businessmen of Cincinnati and the great Ohio River flood of 1884. One of his outstanding works—and still an important reference work for Cincinnati history—is his 1872 volume *Cincinnati Past and Present: or, Its Industrial History as Exhibited in the Life-Labors of Its Leading Men*. His photographs won awards in art competitions in Chicago, Paris, New York, Vienna and London.

But it was his Shakespeare volume that received the most acclaim. The images were framed and hung on the walls of the Shakespeare Memorial Library in Stratford-on-Avon, and the Shakespeare Memorial Association sent him an ornate letter of thanks. In creating the photographs for his *Seven Ages of Man*, Landy took the poetry of Shakespeare's lines and transformed them into images his readers would recognize. For his models he used some actors and actresses who were in Cincinnati at the time, as well as a few local artists and businessmen. His own mother served as the model for the first image of an old nurse holding a baby, and he used himself as the model for the fourth image, the soldier: "Then a soldier, full of strange oaths, and bearded like the pard."

James Landy's book is a beautiful volume, simply and elegantly designed. The cover is a ribbed green cloth with gilded lettering, and each of the sepia photographs is framed and tipped-in on heavy cardstock with Shakespeare's quotable "age" printed on the facing page. The text block is also gilded at the top, bottom and fore edges. Landy's dedication of the volume is to the Irish-born tragedian John McCullough, "in appreciation of his talents as a faithful delineator of Shakespere," a great friend of Landy's and the same John McCullough who would come to a tragic end just a few years later after his performance in the 1883 festival. It was the next year, 1884, that McCullough was on stage in Chicago when he broke down, ranting and slurring his words, and he could not recite his lines. Though the audience thought he was drunk at the time, he was in the final stages of tertiary syphilis and died a few months later in a Philadelphia insane asylum. The years after his death saw a curious legend arise. McCullough's fellow actors held him in such high esteem that in 1889 they erected a statue in his memory in Philadelphia. Having often performed in Washington, D.C., McCullough's legend grew through a tale that he did not die in an asylum but was actually murdered in the wings of the National Theater and buried beneath the stage. To this day, it is said, his ghost haunts the place. The reality of his life and death was much less romantic.

James Landy continued his career for two decades more after the publication of his book, dying of Bright's disease in 1897. He is buried in Spring Grove Cemetery, and the book he created to venerate William Shakespeare's lines is one of the literary treasures of Cincinnati.

Of the celebrated Shakespeareans who traveled to nineteenth-century Cincinnati, Helena Modjeska may have garnered the most attention in the Ohio River Valley. The Polish-born actress was born in Krakow from an affair her mother had with a local nobleman. She achieved quite the renown in her native country but decided to emigrate, and in 1876, Modjeska came to America with her husband and other Polish émigrés with the intent to build a utopian ranch in Anaheim, California. When that venture failed because none of them had the slightest notion of how to run a ranch and the idealism faded, Helena returned to acting, earning acclaim in her roles of Desdemona, Ophelia and Juliet. She first appeared on a Cincinnati stage with Maurice Barrymore in a production of *As You Like It* in 1883, the same year she became an American citizen. Barrymore became the patriarch of a family of actors, father to Lionel, John and Ethel Barrymore, who often acted in Cincinnati in the twentieth century. For Modjeska, Cincinnati was a lucrative stop for her. She returned in 1885 to the Grand Opera House with a repertoire of *As You Like It*, *Twelfth Night* and some light dramas. However, in another tour of Cincinnati in 1897, Helena had a stroke that partially paralyzed her. She decided to remain in Cincinnati until she recovered after several weeks, and then she resumed her tour. Her lasting fame in these parts is through a special Louisville candy, the modjeska. A Louisville confectioner by the name of Anton Busath was smitten with the actress, and he developed a special candy to honor her, a marshmallow dipped in caramel. Soon other Louisville candy makers copied his tribute, and today, modjeskas are identified as a signature Louisville creation.

Over the next several years, Shakespeare productions continued to travel through Cincinnati, again with notable actors such as E.H. Sothern and the Cincinnati-bred actress Julia Marlowe, who would become his wife and acting partner. Born in Caldbeck, England, in 1865, Marlowe's birth name was Sarah Frances Frost. Her father was a shoemaker who ran afoul of the law—or so he thought—in 1869, when Sarah was four years old. During a local horse race, John Frost flicked his whip at another rider. Thinking he had blinded his rival, he packed up his family in a panic and fled to America. The Frosts settled first in Kansas, where John changed the family's last name to Brough and, still unsettled, moved the household again to Portsmouth, Ohio, where it is said that Mrs. Brough operated a rough-and-tumble saloon along the Ohio River that may have also done a side business as a brothel. The Broughs were in Portsmouth for only a few years before they moved downriver to Cincinnati, where Sarah grew up and became known as Fanny Brough. Her mother ran a boardinghouse, and it was there and then that the future tragedienne became enraptured by Shakespeare's plays.

The story is that one day, a traveling book salesman either knocked on the door or was staying in the boardinghouse when he convinced Mrs. Brough to buy a dictionary and a collection of Shakespeare's plays. Sarah seized upon the Shakespeare and carried it with her everywhere, reading the plays, memorizing the lines and planning for an acting career. By her early teens, when she became known as "Fanny," she was playing juvenile roles for a local acting company that toured with Gilbert and Sullivan productions and then had her first Shakespeare role in a presentation of *Romeo and Juliet*, playing the part of Balthazar. Not long after that, Fanny Brough moved to New York, took voice lessons and became "Julia Marlowe." She married a fellow actor by the name of Robert Taber in 1894, and by the next year she was securing roles on Broadway. Just a few years later, Marlowe tired of Taber's jealousy of her career, and they divorced. Over the next decade, she became the foremost Shakespearean actress in America. In 1911, Marlowe married another actor, the renowned Edward Hugh Sothern, and together they formed an acting company that saw them reign as America's acting royalty for the next two decades, even recording scenes from Shakespeare's plays on 78-rpm discs.

Sothern was born in New Orleans, the son of an actor, and raised in England. His two brothers and a sister were also actors, and E.H. began acting with Marlowe in 1904, a few years before they married. Their two signature plays were *Hamlet* and *Romeo and Juliet*. Many times the couple came to Cincinnati, taking in the life of the Bismarck Café, which was the watering hole of choice for touring actors. (Musicians and actors who performed in low comedies tended to gather at the saloon of Irishman Andy Gilligan). One time, Sothern had a bit of Cincinnati drama. As one of the great actors who toured through Cincinnati, in 1901 he was appearing as Hamlet in the Grand Opera House on Vine Street. Another notable actress of the time, Virginia Harned, was playing Ophelia. On the night of January 22, Harned was in the wings with the other actors, waiting for their cues, as Sothern stood on stage to deliver his soliloquy from Act I, Scene 2. He was reciting his lines, "Oh! That this too too solid flesh would melt" when a fire broke out in the theater. Breaking character from the melancholy, indecisive Hamlet, Sothern remained on the stage and calmly directed the audience out of the theater and to safety.

After her move to New York and the establishment of her career, Julia Marlowe often traveled throughout the country, co-starring with her second husband, E.H. Sothern, in many Shakespeare plays, including the role of Ophelia in *Hamlet.*

Cincinnati's great actress Julia Marlowe began her love for Shakespeare as a child in the 1870s when her mother bought a dictionary and an edition of the Bard's plays from a traveling salesman.

During her heyday, Marlowe's celebrity allowed her to earn a fortune both on the stage and off. She made money endorsing practically anything that came her way: shoes and dresses, cigars and cigarettes, beer trays and paper dolls, kitchenware, sheet music and cosmetics. When the couple retired from acting, E.H. often lectured on Shakespeare in the United States and in England and compiled a biography of his wife, while Julia became deeply involved in the suffrage movement, serving on the advisory council of the Congressional Union for Woman Suffrage, and the sale of war bonds during World War I. Together they spent part of each year in Switzerland and part in either New York City; Washington, D.C.; or Marlowe's mansion in the Catskill Mountains. They were married until Sothern died in 1933; Marlowe died in 1950 at the age of eighty-five. Today there is a mural, a small museum room and a historical marker devoted to her in Portsmouth but curiously no indication of her life in Cincinnati, the place where she spent most of her childhood and where she came to love William Shakespeare.

And does a phrase in the University of Cincinnati's alma mater take one of its key phrases from Shakespeare? Who knows for sure? There are so many phrases and words in the common lexicon that were either coined by Shakespeare or appropriated by the Bard that often a Shakespearean phrase is simply in the ear of the beholder. One of those is "Tower of Strength" in the first verse of the song that was composed by local physician Otto Juettner in 1907. In that verse are the words "A fountain of eternal youth, a tower of strength, a rock of truth." Dr. Juettner, a German immigrant in Cincinnati, completed his undergraduate work at Xavier University in 1885 and then earned a degree in 1888 from the Medical College of Ohio, now the University of Cincinnati College of Medicine. Ever devoted to his college days, Juettner wrote the college fight song for Xavier as well as several songs for UC, including the alma mater. And of that song, even

William Howard Taft was moved to say, "It is the finest, most inspiring college song of any I have ever heard."

But, prithee, whence the "tower of strength"? The line is credited as the creation, or at least an adaptation, by William Shakespeare in his play *Richard III*. In the play, King Richard has taken a stand at Bosworth Field to battle the armies of the Earl of Richmond. He has three times the number of soldiers as the future Henry VII, but he has lost his confidence. Informed by the Duke of Norfolk in Act V, Scene 3 that the Earl's armies number only six or seven thousand, Richard responds: "Why, our battalia trebles that account! Besides, the King's name is a tower of strength, Which they upon the adverse faction want." Is that sentiment something a college would desire, given that Richard was soundly defeated—and killed—all because in his words he was in want of a horse?

Some scholars assert that Shakespeare borrowed the line from the Book of Proverbs, 18:10, which states: "The name of the Lord is a strong tower: the righteous runneth into it, and is safe." Be that as it may, the words entered popular parlance after Shakespeare's play and were used frequently to indicate a bastion of character and fortitude. And whether Otto Juettner was a fan of *Richard III* or a close reader of the Bible, it is of no matter now, more than a century after the alma mater's composition. But it is rather nice to lend the authority of both the Bible and the world's greatest playwright to the tune.

Cincinnati continued to build on its long affection for Shakespeare, even during the birth of the film industry, when it offered up its own Cleopatra and Juliet in the person of silent film actress Theda Bara. Born Theodosia Goodman and educated at Walnut Hills High School and the University of Cincinnati, Bara moved to New York with the initial plan of being a stage actress, but quickly embraced the nascent film industry. She played the Shakespeare parts in the 1915 film production of *Romeo and Juliet* and gave a quite lurid portrayal of *Cleopatra* in 1917. She was thirty-one years old when she played the young teen Juliet, and if she had been offered a role as Ophelia then, you could suppose she would have been an appropriate counterpart to the aging Murdoch during his era.

The notion of Shakespeare as extravaganza was embraced by Cincinnati again in 1916, the tercentenary of his death—as it was in the rest of the world—and again in 2016 for the quadricentennial. The University of Cincinnati took up the challenge of commemorating Shakespeare in 1916 with a weeklong festival staged on its campus and in nearby Burnet Woods that included a festival of plays, an Elizabethan market, a parade and songs

In 1916, the English Department put aside literary squabbles to come together in a celebration for the 300th anniversary of Shakespeare's death. The festival was held on campus and in the adjacent Burnet Woods.

and dances. The commemoration was a major event. The Elizabethan market sprang up behind McMicken Hall, Morris dancers performed, there were concerts of period music and folklorists from England were invited to lecture. Recipes of Elizabethan foods were compiled and song sheets distributed. The many events were even filmed for a newsreel that was distributed to theaters and shown before the silent film features. In large measure (for measure), the celebration was a hodgepodge of British culture and eras thought to be germane to William Shakespeare. However accurate or not, it was lively and it was fun. The dances included a demonstration of Morris dancing and what is believed to be the only time an English Department faculty ever fully agreed on doing anything together.

Since then, the decades featured touring plays with the likes of more acting royalty, Alfred Lunt and Lynn Fontanne, Leslie Howard, Katharine Hepburn and Maurice Evans, usually performing at the Taft Theater on Fifth Street. For the most part, the love of Shakespeare took rather an academic path and was seldom a part of public performance. The study of Shakespeare's plays was a prominent aspect of English Department

Hamlet has had some weird and wonderful interpretations and variations over the centuries, and perhaps one of the more remarkable ones was an act created by businessman and ventriloquist William Shakespeare Berger. Berger created the internationally renowned Vent Haven Museum of ventriloquism across the Ohio River from Cincinnati in neighboring Fort Mitchell, Kentucky. In 1942, he worked up a routine based on Act V, Scene 5 from *Hamlet*. *Courtesy of the Vent Haven Museum.*

curricula in both high schools and universities, and at least at the University of Cincinnati, the senior class play was often a Shakespeare work. As you would expect, those were some pretty dry bones.

Those bones took the form of a skull. William Shakespeare Berger was a northern Kentucky businessman who had a passion for ventriloquism and the "vents" that performers used in their acts. These dummies were fascinating to him, so Berger began collecting them, the result of which is today the Vent Haven Museum across the river in Fort Mitchell, Kentucky, and it is the largest such museum in the world. Berger's father named his son after the Bard because of his own passion for his plays. Geza Berger was born in 1842 and became an actor in his native Germany. He immigrated to the United States for what some think were political reasons, and in Cincinnati, he became an editor with the German American press while occasionally acting on the side. Geza's love for Shakespeare carried through in the naming of his son, and young Berger carried it well. As part of his love for ventriloquism, W.S. had some talent of his own. He developed an act in which he stood beside a skull situated on a platform and made it talk. The skull was his Hamlet, and supposedly the eyes would glow during the performance. In the sketch notes that Berger compiled, he begins a conversation with the skull and writes down the special effects: "By Jupiter, you look like Hamlet—lights go out—cock crows—clock dial set at 12—what happened to the lights?" and they see a ghost.

Both Berger father and son carried their Shakespeare to the very end: Geza Berger died in 1930, and his will ends with these words, the final words of Hamlet, Act V, Scene 2: "The rest is silence." William Shakespeare Berger died in 1972, and carved on his tombstone is "The rest is silence."

Another century came along, and in 2016 the 400th anniversary of Shakespeare's death was acknowledged around the world with performances and memorabilia. In the United States, the Folger Shakespeare Library in Washington, D.C., released copies of the 1623 First Folio for exhibit, the seminal volume of Shakespeare's plays, with one appearance in each of the fifty states. The traveling volumes and installations for the nation were coordinated by the Cincinnati Museum Center and included an exhibition titled *Shakespeare and the Queen City* that partnered with the Cincinnati Shakespeare Company, the University of Cincinnati Libraries, Miami University, the Public Library of Cincinnati and Hamilton County and private collections to show the heritage of the city and its affection for Shakespeare. Rare volumes and local playbills were on view along with a stage and costumes so exhibition visitors could catch themselves in the act.

This page: Following the 400th anniversary of Shakespeare's death in 2016, the Cincinnati Museum Center created the exhibit *Cincinnati and the Queen City* in 2017 to show the city's 200-year heritage of performance and literature. With a backdrop of a fairy forest, museum goers could see rare editions of the plays as well as local photographs and ephemera.

In nearby Hamilton, Ohio's Pyramid Hill Sculpture Park is Sam McKinney's beautiful 2010 sculpture *Wherefore Art Thou*. The seventeen-foot bronze and black granite statue depicts Romeo and Juliet's final moments.

With the founding of the Cincinnati Shakespeare Company, the Bard's works truly became part of the city's literary culture again rather than the frequently taught, occasionally performed manifestation it had been since the late nineteenth century. The Company originated as the Fahrenheit Theatre Company in 1993 with the aim of performing Shakespeare for modern audiences. In 1997, Fahrenheit was renamed the Cincinnati Shakespeare Company, and in 2014, CSC became one of the few companies in America to have produced all thirty-eight Shakespeare plays. That number—thirty-eight—also refers to the company's educational outreach program of taking Shakespeare into the schools in Greater Cincinnati to teach acting, production and the stories in the Shakespeare plays and to actively involve students in presenting their own adaptations. With Project38, the summer Shakespeare in the Park programs and its own theater, the Otto M. Budig Theater at the corner of

The Cincinnati Shakespeare Company not only continues the city's long appreciation of Shakespeare but has brought the Bard back to the people as well. With its Project 38 program for Cincinnati schools and its free summer productions in the park, Shakespeare is accessible to everyone.

Elm and Twelfth Streets in Over-the-Rhine that was dedicated in 2017, the Cincinnati Shakespeare Company is very close to sixteenth-century Shakespeare—audiences of everyday people (if not strictly groundlings) along with adaptations and re-workings of the plays.

And in Cincinnati, the groundlings, poets, sinners, playwrights, reporters, cartoonists, various ne'er-do-wells, esteemed authors, not-so-esteemed hacks, satirists, printers, typesetters, ink makers, binders, librarians, archivists and readers still abide.

FIFTEEN ESSENTIAL LITERARY POINTS OF INTEREST

The brick and granite remains of what once was a tribute to the nation's famous authors. It stands close to the 172-foot tall Eden Park standpipe, designed by Samuel Hannaford in 1894.

Authors Grove, Eden Park

Originating in 1882 with the planting of trees on a six-acre section of Eden Park, the Authors Grove had the double intention of educating Cincinnati's schoolchildren about forestry and literature—each tree had a plaque indicating a famous author. Today though, all that remains of the grove is a portion of a brick wall and the concrete form of a book located by the brick water tower.

Carl Blegen Library, University of Cincinnati

Opened in 1930 as the new main library of the university, the building is an art deco treasure with architectural features that illustrate the history of books and reading. There are limestone reliefs of the eminent figures in Eastern and Western civilization, notable printers like Benjamin Franklin, Johannes Gutenberg, Christophe Plantin and William Caxton, bronze reliefs showing the heritage of knowledge, printers' marks both outside and inside the building and bronze chandeliers with proverbs in different languages about the heritage of learning. Rededicated in 1983

One of the forty-one branches of the public library, the Price Hill building is an example of the Carnegie libraries throughout America. The branch was built in 1909 near Dempsey Park at a cost of $26,707.15 and was renovated in 2019 and 2020.

Another piece of public art that honors a literary heritage is the 2012 sculpture of Pinocchio that stands outside the Cincinnati Art Museum. Created by artist Jim Dine and titled *Pinocchio (Emotional)*, the twelve-foot bronze statue was part of the museum's exploration of fairytales in the work of local artists.

and named for Carl Blegen, the eminent archaeologist from UC, the building is located at the south end of campus by Clifton Avenue and Calhoun Street in the Clifton neighborhood.

Carnegie Libraries

Cincinnati had nine Carnegie libraries built between 1905 and 1915, eight of which still survive, with seven of those remaining as libraries. With the variety of distinctive architectural styles mandated by the Carnegie Foundation, they support the neighborhood communities of Price Hill, Cumminsville, Walnut Hills, Corryville, Avondale, Norwood and Hyde Park. The Columbia-Tusculum branch is now the Carnegie Center of Columbia-Tusculum for meetings and cultural events. The Avondale branch is especially notable for its beautiful Rookwood tiles and terra-cotta entrance. And though it is not a Carnegie library, the Clifton branch is located in the historic George B. Cox mansion, the former home of the Cincinnati's early twentieth-century political boss.

Cincinnati Art Museum and Pinocchio

Located on the circle drive at the entrance to the art museum in Eden Park, the giant bronze sculpture of *Pinocchio (Emotional)* was created by artist Jim Dine in 2012. The twelve-foot-high statue of the boy-puppet from Carlo Collodi's 1883 book was unveiled as part of a museum exhibition of fairy tales in the work of Cincinnati artists.

One of the stone sculptures decorating the façade of the art deco Cincinnati Enquirer building at 617 Vine Street. Constructed in 1926, the building now houses two boutique hotels.

Cincinnati Enquirer Building

Constructed in 1926 by the firm of Lockwood Greene, this art deco building housed the newspaper's editorial and publishing divisions. Today, the fourteen-story structure located at 617 Vine Street hosts two boutique hotels, and the exterior still features the limestone grotesques of bookish monks, scribes and printers, along with bronze sculptures illustrating the same book arts but with a classical, toga-clad motif.

Cincinnati Type & Print Museum

This Lower Price Hill museum is at 2307 Eighth Street at the foot of what once was the Price Hill Incline. It was created in 2016 to celebrate the rich heritage of Cincinnati's type foundries and printers, so there are a number of wonderful printing presses and typecases on exhibit. The museum is also a functioning training facility to teach letterpress printing skills for marginalized women in Price Hill and to provide a space for artists to make handmade papers.

Elsinore Tower

Situated on Gilbert Avenue at the foot of Mount Adams and also called the Elsinore Arch, this castle-like building was constructed in 1883. Its function was as a valve house for the Cincinnati Water Works, but its inspiration came from Shakespeare. The Dramatic Festival held in Music Hall in the spring of 1883 presented *Hamlet* with a scenic backdrop of Elsinore Castle that so impressed the Water Works superintendent, who was in the audience, that he commissioned an Elsinore feel for the valve house.

Harriet Beecher Stowe House

Located at 2950 Gilbert Avenue, this historic home is an Ohio History Connection site and open for tours and meetings. Stowe's father, Lyman Beecher, lived here and headed the nearby Lane Theological Seminary. Harriet and her husband, Calvin Stowe, lived in a house near this one, and she visited her father's home frequently, actually giving birth to two of her children here. Her experiences during her Cincinnati years were the inspiration for *Uncle Tom's Cabin*.

Klau Library, Hebrew Union College

Housing the Rabbi David Ellenson Rare Book Room with over fourteen thousand pieces of rare Judaica, incunabula and early printed books, the Klau Library regularly puts its treasures on exhibit. The library is located on the HUC campus at 3101 Clifton Avenue in the neighborhood of Clifton.

Lloyd Library and Museum

The Lloyd Library was founded in the nineteenth century by pharmacist John Uri Lloyd, joined by his fellow pharmacists and brothers Nelson Ashley Lloyd and Curtis Gates Lloyd. The holdings began with their personal research collections in pharmacy, horticulture, medical botany and eclectic medicine. Today, the library and museum, located at 917 Plum Street in downtown Cincinnati, hosts lectures and exhibits related to their rare books and other holdings, and it has expanded the research and collections to include holistic medicine.

Mercantile Library

Founded in 1835 as the Young Men's Mercantile Library Association, the venerable Mercantile Library is the true literary center of Cincinnati. In addition to its collections of contemporary fiction and nonfiction, this membership library hosts a wide range of author talks, lectures, events and study programs, and many of its events are open to nonmembers for a nominal fee. The Mercantile is a historical showpiece of the city with its statuary, architecture and beautiful view atop the downtown area. It is located at 414 Walnut Street.

Otto Budig Theater

Home of the Cincinnati Shakespeare Company, the Budig Theater located at 1195 Elm Street in Over-the-Rhine is a Cincinnati gem. It was built in 2017, and in its modern intimate design,

Fronted by Hamlet the pig, the Otto M. Budig Theater is the home of the Cincinnati Shakespeare Company. Over the past two decades, the company has produced all of Shakespeare's plays, become an educational force in the community and presented free Shakespeare in the Park plays every summer. The beautiful theater at the corner of Twelfth and Elm Streets in Over-the-Rhine is named for Cincinnati businessman and arts philanthropist Otto Budig. In this intimate structure, no seat is more than twenty feet from the stage.

no playgoer is more than twenty feet from the stage. The lobby features the names of all thirty-eight of the Bard's plays on the stairs, and outside is the statue of *HAMlet*, the fiberglass porker from Cincinnati's Big Pig Gig, dressed as the Melancholy Dane.

PUBLIC LIBRARY OF CINCINNATI & HAMILTON COUNTY, MAIN BRANCH

Constructed in 1955 in a modernist design by local architect Woodie Garber, the main branch of the public library has a stark brick exterior that belies an interior of airy spaces in a soaring atrium. The library hosts numerous lectures, and the exhibits, particularly in the History and Genealogy Department, are exceptional looks at Cincinnati heritage. The beautiful stained-glass windows that once adorned an earlier library building in 1874 were reacquired by the PLCH in 2005 and restored for permanent display, one on each floor. In the Joseph S. Stern Jr. Cincinnati Room is one of the world's great series of daguerreotypes, the Cincinnati Panorama of 1848 of the city's waterfront, the work of Charles Fontayne and William S. Porter. Visitors can view these originals on display, and interactive kiosks show high-definition images in which the viewer can zoom in for close looks at the buildings and people along the riverfront and the streets behind it. The plaza entrance at 800 Vine Street is notable for the extraordinary fountain of books, the 1990 Amelia Valerio Weinberg Memorial Fountain created by sculptor Michael Frasca. The water cascading over ceramic books represents the printed word as the flow of inspiration and knowledge.

Detail of the Amelia Valerio Weinberg Memorial Fountain at the main branch of the public library on Vine Street. The fountain was created by sculptor Michael Frasca and dedicated in 1990.

TIMES-STAR BUILDING

Designed by the Samuel Hannaford & Sons architectural firm for the *Times-Star* newspaper, this fifteen-story art deco building at 800 Broadway opened in 1933. Constructed of limestone, the decorative elements are a tribute to the heritage of printing and the history of publishing, in fact, very similar in subject matter to that of Blegen Library at the University of

In the lobby of the Times-Star Building is the mark of sixteenth-century Antwerp printer and publisher Christoph Plantin.

Cincinnati. Exterior reliefs feature exaggerated portrayals of famous printers like Johannes Gutenberg of Germany, Aldus Manutius of Venice, William Caxton of England, Benjamin Franklin of America and others, and there are panel sculptures of printers and typesetters. In the lobby, there are the printers' marks, or trademarks, done in stainless steel of notable printers as well. The building was occupied until 1984, first by the *Times-Star* and subsequently by the *Cincinnati Post*, which purchased its rival. It is now owned by Hamilton County and houses county offices as well as Hamilton Juvenile Court, so while photography of the exterior architecture is unrestricted, the lobby is a secured area and it is advised to ask permission before taking photos of the beautiful printers' marks found there.

Winsor McCay Mural

As part of its mission to create art projects throughout Cincinnati area, the nonprofit ArtWorks Cincinnati employs students under the mentorship of professional artists to paint permanent building murals on a broad variety of subjects. In 2016, a building at 917 Main Street in Over-the-Rhine was used to create a mural honoring pioneering cartoonist and animator Winsor McCay. McCay (1869–1934) came to Cincinnati in 1891 to paint advertisements and backdrops for the city's dime museums and then worked for both the *Cincinnati Enquirer* and the *Commercial Tribune* as an editorial illustrator. In 1903, McCay moved to New York City. The Cincinnati mural extends the full side of the building on Main Street and is a page from his phantasmagorical comic strip, *Little Nemo in Slumberland*, which debuted in the *New York Herald* in 1905 and ran until 1915.

TWENTY-FIVE ESSENTIAL ORGANIZATIONS FOR BOOKS, READING AND WRITING

Adopt a Book
adoptabookohio.org
Nonprofit organization that collects new and gently used books for distribution to schools and programs for disadvantaged children in the Greater Cincinnati area. The goal is to encourage literacy efforts and to foster a love of reading.

Blue Manatee Literacy Project and Bookstore
bluemanatee.org
The Blue Manatee builds the love of literature and reading in children by providing a one-to-one program in which for every book purchased from Blue Manatee, a book is donated so disadvantaged schools that need reading materials can provide them for their students. As part of its "curated literacy" initiative, BMLPB works to help students read at grade level.

Books by the Banks
booksbythebanks.org
BBTB is an annual book festival held each autumn in Cincinnati with national, regional and local authors; panel discussions; workshops; regional information booths; and a children's literary and activities section. The event is sponsored by several local libraries, organizations and businesses.

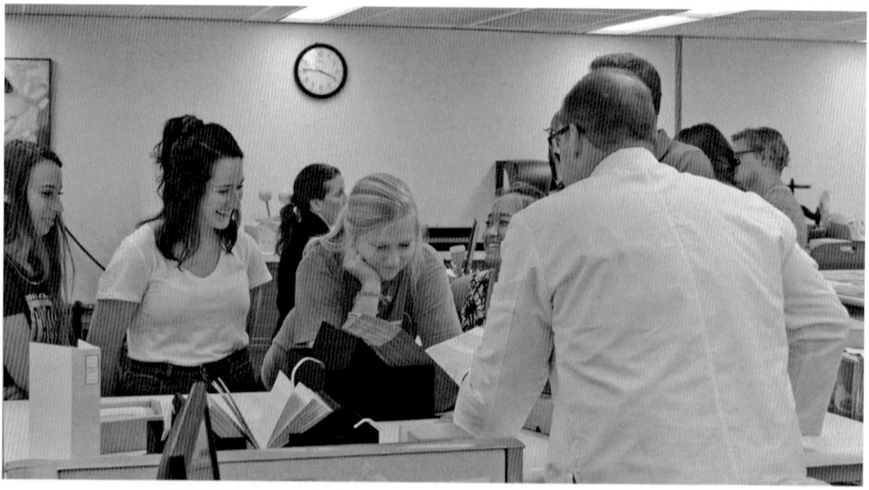

In the Preservation Lab at the University of Cincinnati administered by UC and the public library, students in a global books and reading seminar are shown book treatments by conservation technician Chris Voynovich.

Cincinnati Association for the Blind and Visually Impaired
cincyblind.org
Services for the blind and visually impaired, including talking book machines, talking print, and braille.

Cincinnati Book Arts Society
cincinnatibookarts.org
CBAS is dedicated to promoting and preserving the book arts in all its forms, and every summer it holds the *Bookworks* exhibition at the main branch of the Public Library of Cincinnati and Hamilton County.

Cincinnati Comic Expo
cincinnaticomicexpo.com
Annual event in Cincinnati featuring prominent graphic artists, cartoonists and discussion panels.

Cincinnati Fiction Writers
meetup.com/writers-884
This group brings together writers for critiques and support on their path to being published. It meets the first and third Mondays each month. The meeting locations vary.

Cincinnati Poetry Slam
www.facebook.com/events/artsville/cincinnati-poetry-slam/326476307874974
The CPS invites contemporary performance poets to read their work in competition and sponsors regular events, providing a dynamic urban aspect to local literature.

Cincinnati Shakespeare Company
cincyshakes.com
CincyShakes is a professional theater company that not only performs Shakespeare plays but the classics as well, and contemporary plays are often a part of their seasons. In their community outreach, CSC has a free summer Shakespeare in the Park program that presents two to three different Shakespeare plays in parks throughout the Greater Cincinnati area. The company also has a program called Project38 in which the actors go into schools to help students and teachers bring the plays to life.

Cincy Children's Book Writers & Illustrators
www.facebook.com/pg/CincyKidWriters/about/?ref=page_internal
This group meets on a regular basis, providing information, feedback and support for a growing community of illustrators.

Friends of the Public Library of Cincinnati and Hamilton County
cincylibraryfriends.org
The Friends group supports the programs, collections and activities of the public library. It maintains a shop inside the main branch of the library in downtown Cincinnati as well as a warehouse for donations and a bookstore in the suburban neighborhood of Hartwell. The Friends also sponsor regular public book sales.

Greater Cincinnati Writers League
cincinnatiwritersleague.org
An organization that has been around for nearly a century, the League originally formed in 1930 for writers and musicians to talk about their work. Membership is limited to sixty people, but visitors to monthly meetings can listen in on sessions, held at the Hermitage Room of the Regency, 2444 Madison Road.

Literacy Network of Greater Cincinnati
lngc.org; www.facebook.com/LNGCCincy
Working with eight counties in the Cincinnati area, the network's mission is to foster literacy in schools, in businesses and in homes. It regularly gathers books for donation to schools and has provided more than fifty Little Free Libraries throughout the area.

Lloyd Library and Museum
lloydlibrary.org; www.facebook.com/LloydLibrary
Established by pharmacist brothers John Uri Lloyd, Nelson Ashley Lloyd and Curtis Gates Lloyd in the late 1800s, this private library is open to the public. Collecting rare books, contemporary books and journals about botany, pharmacy, natural history and medicine, it regularly hosts exhibits and lectures.

The Mercantile Library of Cincinnati
mercantilelibrary.com
Founded in 1835 as the Young Men's Mercantile Library Association, the venerable Mercantile Library is the true literary center of Cincinnati. In addition to its collections of contemporary fiction and nonfiction, this membership library hosts a wide range of author talks, lectures, events and study programs, and many of its events are open to nonmembers for a nominal fee. The Mercantile is a historical showpiece of the city with its statuary, architecture and beautiful view atop the downtown area. It is located at 414 Walnut Street.

Ohio Center for the Book
ohiocenterforthebook.org
Sure, the Ohio Center for the Book is hours away from Cincinnati, located in the Cleveland Public Library, but its celebration of books and reading, and libraries and literature, is vital for all Ohioans. The center is the designated Ohio affiliate of the Library of Congress Center for the Book. It was established in 1997 to promote the literary heritage of Ohio and houses a growing collection of works by Ohio authors, so it is important to Cincinnatians too. The Ohio Center for the Book is also notable for its embrace of graphic novels and literary cartooning. Of course, Superman is a native Ohioan, born in Cleveland rather than on Krypton. The center is located at 325 Superior Avenue in Cleveland.

Ohioana Library Association

ohioana.org

Located in Columbus, the Ohioana Library Association was founded in 1929 and collects books, sheet music and archival items of Ohio authors. Ohioana also sponsors book talks and exhibits, an annual book festival in Columbus and Ohio author recognition awards through the state's county libraries.

Over-the-Rhine Learning Center

otrlearningcenter.org

The goal of the OTR Learning Center is to make it easier for adults in the neighborhood to achieve literacy. As part of this, it offers a basic reading program, an introduction to computers and preparation for earning a GED.

Poet Laureate Program, City of Cincinnati

cincinnati-oh.gov/mayor/cincinnati-poet-laureate

Initiated by the Office of the Mayor in Cincinnati, the poet laureate program began in 2016. The appointed laureate serves a two-year term and works to promote the reading and writing of poetry as well as composing and reading poetry at special events.

Semi-Colon Club

stowehousecincy.org/semi-colon-club.html.

This venerable literary club was formed in the mid-nineteenth century, its membership at that time including local writers. Harriet Beecher Stowe was a member from 1832 to 1850, and it is the historic property of the Harriet Beecher Stowe House in Cincinnati that now co-sponsors many of the club's public talks on women's history, social justice and contemporary issues.

State Library of Ohio

library.ohio.gov

Another organization outside the Cincinnati area but vitally important in the city's literary efforts, the state library in Columbus serves all Ohio libraries and citizens with print and digital collections and literacy programs.

Under Cover Book Club

undercover513.com

This unusual club is a book-based scavenger hunt in Cincinnati, Ohio, that posts location clues on social media to find the books hidden around the city.

The books are typically contemporary and popular novels. Its purpose is to foster literary camaraderie among Cincinnati readers.

Women Writing for (A) Change
womenwriting.org
Founded in 1991 by Mary Pierce Brosmer, a Cincinnati poet and teacher, the intent of this organization is provide an encouraging and supportive framework for women to share their voices and their lives through writing. It offers classes, workshops and writing circles.

WordPlay Cincy
wordplaycincy.org
Located in the neighborhood of Northside, this organization helps children and teens share their voices through the spoken word and through writing about their lives. Through its programs in storytelling, writing and reading that build academic skills, WordPlay's intent is to break the cycle of poverty.

Writer-in-Residence Program, Public Library of Cincinnati & Hamilton County
cincinnatilibrary.org/programs/writerinresidence
Initiated in 2016 by the Library Foundation, the public library's writer-in-residence program appoints a local writer to the position each year to serve as a literary ambassador to Cincinnati and engage in local literary events. The Writer-in-Residence engages with readers and writers with in-person consultations and online support about the writing craft.

A final Cincinnati printing block.

FIFTY ESSENTIAL BOOKS FOR UNDERSTANDING CINCINNATI

Baskin, John, and Lonnie Wheeler. *The Cincinnati Game.* Wilmington, OH: Orange Frazer Press, 1988.

Brown, Dale Patrick. *Brilliance and Balderdash: Early Lectures at Cincinnati's Mercantile Library.* Cincinnati, OH: Mercantile Library, 2007.

———. *Literary Cincinnati: The Missing Chapter.* Athens: Ohio University Press, 2011.

Campbell, Polly. *Cincinnati Food: A History of Queen City Cuisine.* Charleston, SC: The History Press, 2020.

Cist, Charles. *Cincinnati in 1841: Its Early Annals and Future Prospects.* Cincinnati: Charles Cist, 1841.

Clubbe, John. *Cincinnati Observed: Architecture and History*. Columbus: Ohio State University Press, 1992.

Dabney, Wendell P. *Cincinnati's Colored Citizens: Historical, Sociological and Biographical.* Cincinnati, OH: Dabney Publishing, 1926.

Dannenbaum, Jed. *Drink and Disorder: Temperance Reform in Cincinnati from the Washingtonian Revival to the WCTU.* Urbana: University of Illinois Press, 1984.

Day, David, and Barbara Day. *Vanishing Cincinnati.* Wilmington, OH: Orange Frazer Press, 2012.

Drake, Daniel. *Natural and Statistical View, or Picture of Cincinnati and the Miami Country.* Cincinnati, OH: Looker and Wallace, 1815.

DuSablon, Mary Anna. *Cincinnati Recipe Treasury: The Queen City's Culinary Heritage.* Athens: Ohio University Press, 1989.

———. *Walking the Steps of Cincinnati*. rev. ed. Athens: Ohio University Press, 2014. Originally published 1998.

Fleischman, John. *Free & Public: One Hundred and Fifty Years at the Public Library of Cincinnati & Hamilton County, 1853–2003*. Wilmington, OH: Orange Frazer Press, 2003.

Flischel, Robert A., Anita J. Ellis, and Walter E. Langsam. *An Expression of the Community: Cincinnati Public Schools' Legacy of Art and Architecture*. Cincinnati, OH: Art League Press, 2001.

Fortin, Roger. *Faith and Action: A History of the Archdiocese of Cincinnati, 1821–1996*. Columbus: Ohio State University Press, 2002.

———. *Fellowship: History of the Cincinnati Irish*. Cincinnati, OH: Friendly Sons of St. Patrick Foundation, 2018.

Fox, John, ed. *Transforming Cincinnati: How a Decade of ArtWorks Murals Changed People and Communities Forever*. Wilmington, OH: Orange Frazer Press, 2017.

Franklin, Diana Britt. *The Good-Bye Door: The Incredible True Story of America's First Female Serial Killer to Die in the Chair*. Kent, OH: Kent State University Press, 2008.

Gerstacker, Friedrich. *"The El Dorado of the German Emigrant," Writings About the Queen City of the West*. Translated by Don Heinrich Tolzmann. Indianapolis, IN: NCSA Literatur, 2020.

Giglierno, Geoffrey J., Deborah A. Overmyer and Frederic L. Propas. *The Bicentennial Guide to Greater Cincinnati: A Portrait of Two Hundred Years*. Cincinnati, OH: Cincinnati Historical Society, 1988.

Goss, Charles Frederic. *Cincinnati, the Queen City, 1788–1912*, 4 vols. Chicago: S.J. Clarke Publishing, 1912.

Harlow, Alvin F. *The Serene Cincinnatians*. New York: E.P. Dutton and Company, 1950.

Hearn, Lafcadio. *Children of the Levee*. Edited by O.W. Frost. Lexington: University of Kentucky Press, 1957.

Holian, Timothy J. *Over the Barrel: The Brewing History and Beer Culture of Cincinnati*. 2 vols. Cincinnati, OH: Sudhaus Press, 2000 and 2001.

Hurley, Daniel. *Cincinnati: The Queen City*. Cincinnati, OH: Cincinnati Historical Society, 1982.

Juettner, Otto. *Daniel Drake and His Followers: Historical and Biographical Sketches*. Cincinnati, OH: Harvey Publishing, 1909.

Leonard, John W. *The Centennial Review of Cincinnati: One Hundred Years of Progress in Commerce, Manufactures, the Professions, and in Social and Municipal Life*. Cincinnati, OH: J.M. Elstner, 1888.

Mecklenborg, Jacob R. *Cincinnati's Incomplete Subway: The Complete History.* Charleston, SC: The History Press, 2010.

Morgan, Michael. *Cincinnati Beer.* Charleston, SC: The History Press, 2019.

———. *Over-the-Rhine: When Beer Was King.* Charleston, SC: The History Press, 2010.

Niehoff, Buck. *Something Funny at the Library.* Cincinnati, OH: Mercantile Library, 2004.

O'Brien, Donald C. *The Engraving Trade in Early Cincinnati, With a Brief Account of the Lithographic Trade.* Athens: Ohio University Press, 2013.

Perry, Dick. *Vas You Ever in Zinzinnati?* Garden City, NY: Doubleday & Co., 1966.

Roma, Catherine, Craig Doolin, Karin Pendle and Frank Pendle. *A City That Sings: Cincinnati's Choral Tradition 1800–2012.* Wilmington, OH Orange Frazer Press, 2012.

Shotwell, John B. *A History of the Schools of Cincinnati.* Cincinnati, OH: School Life Company, 1902.

Stanforth, Sherry Cook, and Richard Hague, eds. *Riparian: Poetry, Short Prose, and Photographs Inspired by the Ohio River.* Loveland, OH: Dos Madres Press, 2019.

Stradling, David. *In Service to the City: A History of the University of Cincinnati.* Cincinnati, OH: University of Cincinnati Press, 2018.

Suess, Jeff. *AAC150: Make Art, Make a Difference.* Cincinnati, OH: Art Academy of Cincinnati, 2018.

———. *Cincinnati: An Illustrated Timeline.* St. Louis, MO: Reedy Press, 2020.

Sutton, Walter. *The Western Book Trade: Cincinnati as a 19th Century Publishing & Book-Trade Center.* Columbus: Ohio State University Press, 1961.

Tallmadge, John. *The Cincinnati Arch: Learning from Nature in the City.* Athens: University of Georgia Press, 2004.

Taylor, Nikki. *Frontiers of Freedom: Cincinnati's Black Community, 1802–1868.* Athens: Ohio University Press, 2005.

Tolzmann, Don Heinrich. *Over-the-Rhine Tour Guide: Cincinnati's Historic German District, Over-the-Rhine, and Environs.* Milford, OH: Little Miami Publishing, 2011.

Tracy, Steven C. *Going to Cincinnati: A History of the Blues in the Queen City.* Urbana: University of Illinois Press, 1998.

Venable, W.H. *Beginnings of Literary Culture in the Ohio Valley: Historical and Biographical Sketches.* Cincinnati, OH: Robert Clarke & Company, 1891.

Vitz, Robert C. *At the Center: 175 Years at Cincinnati's Mercantile Library.* Cincinnati, OH: Mercantile Library, 2010.

———. *The Queen & The Arts: Cultural Life in Nineteenth-Century Cincinnati.* Kent, OH: Kent State University Press, 1989.

Woellert, Dann. *Cincinnati Goetta: A Delectable History.* Charleston, SC: The History Press, 2019.

———. *Cincinnati Turner Societies: The Cradle of an American Movement.* Charleston, SC: The History Press, 2012.

Writers' Program of the Works Progress Administration of Ohio. *Cincinnati, A Guide to the Queen City and Its Neighbors.* Cincinnati, OH: Wiesen-Hart Press, 1943.

NOTES

1. Douglas C. McMurtrie, *Antecedent Experience in Kentucky of William Maxwell, Ohio's First Printer* (Louisville, KY: n.p., 1932).
2. Stephen Gutgesell, *Guide to Ohio Newspapers, 1793–1973* (Columbus: Ohio Historical Society, 1974).
3. *Trubner's Bibliographical Guide to American Literature* (London: Trubner & Company, 1855).
4. John Milton, *Areopagitica; A Speech of Mr. John Milton for the Liberty of Unlicenc'd Printing, to the Parlament of England* (London: n.p., 1644).
5. Wanda L. Boaz, "The History of the American Book Company Prior to 1900" (undergraduate paper, Ohio University, 1978).
6. Christopher Morley, *Parnassus on Wheels* (Garden City, NY: Doubleday, Page & Company, 1917).
7. *Laws and Regulations of the Cincinnati College* (Cincinnati, OH: Cooke, Powers and Penney, 1819).
8. Reginald C. McGrane, *The University of Cincinnati: A Success Story in Urban Higher Education* (New York: Harper & Row, 1963).
9. Louis L. Tucker, "The Semi-Colon Club of Cincinnati" *Ohio History Journal* 73 (1966).
10. Jack P. de Vise, *A Magnificent Heritage: 150 Years of Scottish Rite Freemasonry in the Valley of Cincinnati* (Cincinnati, OH: Valley of Cincinnati, 2003).
11. *A Catalogue of Select Books, Comprising a Number of Very Desirable Items from the Library of the Late Enoch T. Carson* (Cincinnati, OH: U.P. James, Bookseller, 1902).

12. Virginius C. Hall, *Reflections in the HALLway: A Memoir of the Early Years* (Fort Thomas, KY: MicroPress, 2017).
13. *Blue Law Ballads: A Purge for Puritans by the Sinner,* (Cincinnati, OH: Wm. C. Smith, 1922).
14. William H. Venable, ed., *Poems of William Haines Lytle* (Cincinnati, OH: Robert Clarke Company, 1894).
15. George Elliston, *Changing Moods* (Cincinnati, OH: Sign of the Pen and Pad, 1922).
16. Charles Dickens, *American Notes for General Circulation* (London: Chapman & Hall, 1842).
17. Jon C. Hughes, *The Tanyard Murder: On the Case with Lafcadio Hearn* (Washington, D.C.: University Press of America, 1982).
18. Dorothy V. Martin, "The Truth About Cincinnati's First Library," *Ohio State Archaeological and Historical Society Quarterly* 53 (July–September 1944).
19. *History of the Young Men's Mercantile Library Association of Cincinnati, 1835–1935* (Cincinnati, OH: n.p., 1935).
20. *The Literary Club of Cincinnati, 1849–1949, Centennial Book* (Cincinnati, OH: n.p., 1949).
21. Eira Tansey, "Branches from the Baron: Cincinnati's Carnegie Libraries," *Ohio Valley History* 16, no. 1 (2016); Mary Ellen Armentrout, *Carnegie Libraries of Ohio: Our Cultural Heritage* (Wellington, OH: self-published, 2003).
22. Elizabeth W. Garber, *Implosion: A Memoir of an Architect's Daughter* (Berkeley, CA: She Writes Press, 2018).
23. N.M. Ludlow, *Dramatic Life as I Found It* (St. Louis, MO: G.I. Jones and Company, 1880).
24. Fanny Trollope, *Domestic Manners of the Americans* (London: Whitaker, Treacher & Company, 1832).
25. Olive Logan, *Before the Footlights and Behind the Scenes: A Book About "The Show Business" In All Its Branches…Seen from Within Through the Eyes of the Former Actress* (Philadelphia: Parmelee & Company, 1870).
26. James Landy, *Shakspere's* [sic] *Seven Ages of Man, Illustrated with Photographs from Life* (Cincinnati, OH: Robert Clarke & Company, 1876).

INDEX

ABOUT THE AUTHOR

Kevin Grace is the head of the Archives and Rare Books Library at the University of Cincinnati and the University Archivist. He also teaches in the University Honors Program on the global culture of books and reading, Shakespeare, folklore and mythology, rare books and manuscripts and Irish America. Grace is the author or coauthor of more than a dozen books on Cincinnati. In 2015, he was awarded the Cooper Award by the Public Library of Cincinnati and Hamilton County for contributions to the promotion of books and reading. Grace is also the creator of two Facebook pages, Guide to Literary Cincinnati and Cincinnati Shakespeare Heritage, and his research has taken him around the world to more than two dozen countries. He strongly believes in the power of reading aloud and that homes empty of books are empty houses.